EUROPEAN AND DECORATIONS
TO 1945

Peter Duckers

SHIRE PUBLICATIONS

First published in Great Britain in 2008 by Shire Publications Ltd,
Midland House, West Way, Botley, Oxford OX2 0PH, United Kingdom.
443 Park Avenue South, New York, NY 10016, USA.

E-mail: shire@shirebooks.co.uk   •   www.shirebooks.co.uk

A CIP catalog record for this book is available from the British Library.

Shire Library no. 463   •   ISBN-13: 978 0 7478 0670 7

Peter Duckers has asserted his right under the Copyright, Designs and Patents Act, 1988, to be identified as the author of this book.

Designed by Ken Vail Graphic Design, Cambridge, UK and typeset in Perpetua and Gill Sans. Printed in Malta by Gutenberg Press Ltd.

08 09 10 11 12   10 9 8 7 6 5 4 3 2 1

COVER IMAGE
Italy: Breast Star and Neck Badge of the Military Order of Savoy (see page 54).

TITLE PAGE IMAGE
Great Britain: Royal Victorian Order. Set of insignia of the First Class (Grand Cross or GCVO). The design simply features the 'VRI' cipher of Queen Victoria as Queen and Empress of India and her name as founder.

CONTENTS PAGE IMAGE
France: Order of the Holy Ghost. Part of the Chain or Collar of the Grand Cross. Since these were awarded only to persons of the highest status, their workmanship is usually of the very finest standard. The Chain shown here is an example of exquisite craftsmanship in enamelwork in miniature.

ACKNOWLEDGEMENTS
The author wishes to express his thanks to the collectors and organisations who have provided illustrations for this work, including Messrs. Spink and Son of Southampton Row, Bloomsbury, London and Messrs DNW of Bolton Street, Piccadilly, London.

He particularly wishes to acknowledge the contribution of the auctioneers Messrs. Morton and Eden of 45, Maddox Street, London, without whose generous assistance it would not have been possible to illustrate many of the Orders in this work.

CONTENTS

INTRODUCTION	5
THE ORDERS	14
Albania	14
Andorra	15
Austria	15
Belgium	19
Bohemia	21
Bulgaria	21
Burgundy	23
Byzantine Empire	24
Courland	24
Croatia	24
Czechoslovakia	25
Denmark	26
Ephemeral or International Orders	28
Estonia	29
Finland	29
France	31
Germany: the German States	36
Germany: the German Empire	37
Germany: the Third Reich	38
Great Britain	41

Greece   47
The Holy Land   49
Hungary   50
Iceland   51
Ireland   52
Italy: the Italian States   52
Italy   52
Latvia   56
Liechtenstein   57
Lithuania   57
Luxembourg   58
Malta   60
Monaco   61
Montenegro   62
The Netherlands   63
Norway   65
Poland   66
Portugal   67
Prussia   71
Romania   73
The Russian Empire   76
San Marino   81
Serbia   82
Slovakia   85
Sovereign Orders   85
Spain   85
Sweden   91
Switzerland   93
Turkey   93
Ukraine   96
The Union of Soviet Socialist Republics   96
The Vatican   103
Yugoslavia   105

FURTHER READING   108

COLLECTING ORDERS AND DECORATIONS   111

INDEX   112

INTRODUCTION

O RDERS of Chivalry or Knighthood were royal or noble associations established by European ruling houses and princely families from the early Middle Ages onwards. Admission to them was intended to reinforce the bonds of allegiance between the ruler and powerful magnates or to provide a prestigious reward for loyal service. These confraternities had their own Statutes (rules of conduct and governance), their own livery, their own officials and usually their own chapel or dedicated place of assembly. Their badges – 'Orders' in medallic or numismatic terms – were worn to show that their recipient was a member of a particular Order of Knighthood at a particular grade.

An example of a group of European awards (left to right): Swedish Order of the Sword, 'with swords' (Knight); Swedish Order of the Pole Star (Knight); Swedish medal for the 1912 Olympics; Russian Order of St Anne, Third Class; French Legion of Honour (Officer).

(Below left to right)
Italy: Order of the Annunciation. In their fitted case of award, the magnificent Collar, pendant Badge and Breast Star, by Cravanzola of Rome, c.1915.

Romania: Order of St Michael the Brave. The unusual Breast Badge takes the form of a light-blue enamelled cross flory. In the centre is the cipher of King Ferdinand I, who founded the Order in 1916. The Order has no associated Breast Star.

Greece: Order of the Redeemer. Officer's Breast Badge in gold and enamel; this is the first type (1833–62), bearing the profile of King Otto I.

As the Middle Ages passed and country landowners replaced warrior aristocrats, the conferring of an Order became a way of rewarding important political or military service to the monarch or state, and in modern times Orders continue to fulfil this purpose, far removed from medieval notions of chivalry or feudal service.

Few European countries have no system of Orders (though Andorra and Switzerland are examples) and even in non-European and post-colonial nations, such as those of modern Africa, Orders have been retained or even created in modern times and continue to be conferred as highly regarded rewards for service to the state.

BADGES

The Badges of an Order are normally made in bullion metals – platinum, gold or silver – and colourful enamels. Since they are designed to be prestigious awards at any grade, they are usually of high-quality materials and workmanship and some are of exquisite design; they are intended to be beautiful, decorative jewels as much as medals.

Most are based on a cross shape, using every conceivable type – Maltese, Greek, Lorraine, Geneva – or in every heraldic variation, pattée, saltire, flory, etc. They are worn, according to class, on the hip from a wide sash or around the neck from a ribbon (cravat) or on the breast from a ribbon.

The Badges may be larger or smaller depending on the class of award. They usually depict on the *obverse* (front) centre subjects such as the ruling

monarch, the Order's founder, the country's patron saint or other holy image, symbolic mythological figures, heroes from the nation's past, or simply the monarch's cipher or a national emblem. The *reverse* (back) centre often has a national emblem or the ruler's emblem or cipher, the year of foundation or some other significant date.

Awards to military or naval recipients for war service frequently have crossed swords as an element of the design and some are worn on distinctive military ribbons (e.g. Serbian Orders for 1914–18, q.v.).

The Badges are suspended from their ribbons in a variety of ways – most commonly from a simple ring, but sometimes from a crown or (often in the case of awards for war service) from crossed swords. Others may have an eagle, a wreath (e.g. the French Legion of Honour), a trophy of arms or some other decorative device.

BREAST STARS

Breast Stars are worn with the first and second classes of most Orders and are generally carried on the left breast. Before about 1850 they were often made of cloth or bullion wire and simply stitched on to the jacket or uniform. From the mid nineteenth century metal stars became the norm. They are

(Left) Austria: Order of Military Merit. Neck Badge in silver-gilt and enamel of the Second Class, 'with wreath and swords', indicating an award for war service.

(Right) An example of Orders being worn: Breast Badge of the Order of Vasa, Sweden, and Neck Badge and Breast Star of St Anne, Russia.

(Left) France: Order of St Lazarus of Jerusalem and Our Lady of Mount Carmel. A late-eighteenth-century bullion wire Breast Star of a Knight.

(Right) The back of a Breast Star, showing the typically plain reverse with the long pin fastening by which it is attached to the uniform or jacket.

usually in silver or white metal and often take the form of an eight-pointed star, a rayed cross or a starburst, and they commonly carry the obverse of the Badge of the Order in their centre, or some design element taken from it. Privately commissioned types are sometimes seen set with diamonds or other gems. The reverse is usually plain and fitted with a long pin or screw fastening to allow the Star to be attached to the uniform or jacket.

GRADES OR CLASSES

There is considerable variation in the organisation of Orders into grades or classes. Put simply, the higher the class, the more prestigious the award. European Orders often have more classes or divisions than do British types, but a typical arrangement is in five classes:

> *Grand Cross, or First Class*: wears a wide Sash over the left or right shoulder, carrying the insignia (Badge) of the award at the hip, and a Breast Star.
>
> *Knight Commander, or Second Class*: wears a Breast Star and the Badge of the Order around the neck.
>
> *Commander, or Third Class*: wears the Badge of the Order around the neck.
>
> *Officer, or Fourth Class*: wears the Badge on a ribbon at the breast, along with other Orders and medals. With some European Orders, a rosette or cockade on the ribbon identifies this grade.
>
> *Knight, or Fifth Class*: wears the Badge on a ribbon at the breast, along with other Orders and medals. There is no cockade on the ribbon and the Badge is often slightly smaller or of a different metal (e.g. silver rather than gold).

(Left) Spain: Royal and Military Order of Maria Christina. Late-nineteenth-century Breast Star of the Grand Cross (First Class), Military Division, with the central legend *Al merito en campagna* ('For merit on campaign' or 'in the field').

(Right) An example of Orders being worn – a Swedish officer of *c*.1910. He wears at his neck the Russian Order of St Stanislas, Second Class, and on his breast the Swedish Order of the Sword, the Russian Order of St Anne, the French Legion of Honour, the British medal for the Boer War and the Swedish Order of the Pole Star.

Some European Orders have more classes than this and may subdivide classes into grades (e.g. Second Class, First Grade). Sometimes differences in class are identified by Badges that vary in size (the higher the class, the larger the Badge, as with the French Legion of Honour), or by wider ribbons, added ribbon stripes or ribbon emblems. Some have a higher grade in the form of a Collar or Chain and others have Medals (sometimes with separate classes, commonly gold, silver or bronze) associated with them as lower-tier awards for persons of lesser rank or for lesser achievements.

In addition, it is common to distinguish military or war service awards from civil. The former usually have crossed sword devices through the Badge itself, or as part of its suspension, or as emblems on the ribbon.

Promotion to a higher grade of an Order usually requires the surrender of the lower-tier insignia; insignia of different grades are not usually worn together, though they may be if one award is for military and the other for civil service.

In many instances, especially with the higher grades of an Order, the insignia have to be returned to the state on the death of the recipient, so that official awards at these grades rarely appear on the collectors' market. Also, some Orders have strict limits on the number of holders, especially at the highest grades, and examples of their insignia are rarely seen. However, since the insignia of many European awards may be privately purchased (see below) or replaced by personally commissioned pieces, examples of the different grades may sometimes be found.

The statutes of most Orders require the surrender of the insignia and removal (*erasure*) from the Register of the Order, with the public disgrace attendant on it, if the recipient is deemed to have brought dishonour to

(Below) Prussia: Royal House Order of Hohenzollern. Neck Badge of a Grand Commander, 'with swords'.

The typical order of wearing the different grades of Orders (left to right): First Class – Sash, Sash Badge and Breast Star; Second Class – Neck Badge and Breast Star; Third Class – Neck Badge. Fourth and Fifth Classes are worn as Breast Badges, alongside other decorations and medals. A ribbon rosette commonly differentiates the Fourth Class from the Fifth.

the Order – for example, by being convicted of treason or some other major crime.

RIBBONS AND EMBLEMS

With the exception of insignia worn only as pin-back or screw-back Breast Badges (e.g. many wartime Soviet awards), Badges are worn from distinctive coloured ribbons and some have variations according to grade or for military and civil divisions. It is therefore possible to identify a person's award and grade if the recipient is simply wearing a strip of ribbons.

A group to a Swedish recipient, with a fine array of Orders and Medals (left to right): Swedish Royal Order of the Sword (Knight); Medal for the Stockholm Olympics, 1912; Danish Order of Dannebrog (Knight, Christian X suspension); Finnish Mannerheim Cross of the Order of Liberty (Fourth Class, with military ribbon emblem); Finnish Order of the White Rose (Fifth Class): Finnish War Medal, 1939–40; Prussian Order of the Red Eagle, Fourth Class; French Academic Palms (Officer).

There are variations in the way that ribbons are worn from a Breast Badge. It was traditional, for example, in the Austrian, Greek, Serbian and Bulgarian systems to wear ribbons folded into a triangle; in some German states they were folded into a horseshoe or oval shape, and in Russia into a pentagon. They may also be worn as bows, usually by female recipients.

Many European states employ ribbon emblems as a simple method of indicating different classes, distinctions or services. Crossed swords on the ribbon may indicate an award for military service, but there are also palm leaves, silver or gilt stars, wreaths of oak or laurel, anchors (for naval service) and others.

A common feature of European awards, not reflected in the British system, is the wearing of rosettes or cockades on the ribbon. These are used primarily to denote a different grade; it is common for the Fourth Class of an Order (e.g. the Order of the Redeemer of Greece or the French Legion of Honour) to carry a rosette on the medal ribbon while the lower Fifth Class does not.

MINIATURES
Miniature versions of the Badges (though not Breast Stars) may be privately purchased from manufacturers or jewellers. These are worn in evening dress or on formal occasions in place of the heavier originals. In some European countries these miniatures, whose materials and quality may vary according to date, producer or cost, are worn not from reduced ribbons of the Order

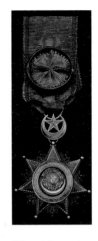

(Above) A rosette on the ribbon of the Ottoman Order of the Osmanieh. A rosette is commonly used on European orders to designate the Fourth Class of a Badge. Lower classes might have no rosette or be in a lesser metal (silver rather than gold) or be slightly smaller in size.

(Below) A miniature group worn in the British fashion on reduced ribbons. It has the MBE, three medals for 1914–18, and four foreign orders worn, as usual, at the end of the British set. They are (left to right): the Romanian Order of the Crown, the Serbian Order of the White Eagle 'with swords', the Polish Order of Military Virtue, and the Serbian Order of the Karageorge Star 'with swords'. All are of the Fourth Class, indicated by ribbon rosettes.

A Russian miniature group, worn 'continental style' from a gold chain, as commonly seen with European examples. It comprises (left to right): the Orders of St Andrew, St Alexander Nevsky, the White Eagle, St Vladimir (in black), St Anne, and a medal for the Turkish war of 1828–29.

(as in Britain) but without a ribbon, suspended from gold or silver chains, rather in the manner of pocket-watch chains and fobs.

MANUFACTURERS AND TYPES

The insignia are manufactured by the country's official mint or, very commonly, by established jewellers or specialist firms. Most are discreetly hallmarked and/or marked with their manufacturer's details. It follows that there may be variations in detail, in materials and in quality from manufacturer to manufacturer or across long periods of time. Some insignia have been created by the most celebrated court jewellers – examples of Russian Orders created by Fabergé, for example, are highly collected and appropriately expensive. (For details of the various manufacturers of Orders, see: *Court Jewellers of theWorld* by J. R. Jacob, New Jersey, 1978.)

Unlike the British system, in some European countries it is common for the recipient of an Order to purchase the insignia rather than receive an

(Left) Examples of hallmarks. Most Orders carry a variety of marks indicating fineness of metal, maker's initials, date and place of manufacture, etc. They are usually very small and discreetly placed. These are on the reverse of the Collar Chain of a Russian Order.

(Centre) An example of a jewel-set 'private commission', in this case a late-eighteenth-century Badge of the Russian Order of St Anne. Since most

recipients were men of wealth and status, such elaborately personalised versions were presumably affordable. Compare with the usual version of this Badge on page 78.

(Right) A modern version of an ancient Order, in this case the Sash Badge of the First Class of the French Order of the Holy Spirit. Since original insignia of early Orders are rarely seen, modern pieces have been manufactured for collectors and museums.

official issue. These 'private purchase' types can vary in quality of manufacture and in small details. Similarly, some recipients prefer to have more elaborate Badges than the standard types and may commission from leading jewellers pieces in better-quality enamels or set with precious stones – or whatever they can afford.

There are therefore more variations in design, materials and workmanship with European Orders than there tend to be with the more standardised British awards. Equally, some early or rare insignia (e.g. early French awards) have been privately produced in modern times specifically to supply the collectors' or museum market. And, as in all fields of antiques and collecting, there are fakes and copies produced with the intention to deceive. No field is more fraught with danger in this respect than the awards of Nazi Germany. The collector must decide what he or she considers to be acceptable – an official award, a jeweller's version, an idiosyncratic commission, a modern reproduction or an outright fake.

PRESENTATION

In most cases the recipient receives an elaborate bestowal document or document of appointment to the Order and a copy of its current statutes. The insignia are usually presented in fitted cases.

The actual presentation of most awards used to take place in circumstances of great pomp and ceremony and where possible they were conferred by the monarch or head of state in person. This sometimes still occurs, especially with the highest grades and the most prestigious Orders. But in these days of often large-scale awards at the lower levels of some Orders it is just as common for the insignia to be presented locally by some other dignitary (town mayor, military commander, etc) or simply sent by post.

(Left) An example of an Order in a fitted case of issue. The Breast Star and Badge of the Russian Order of St Anne, First Class, 'with swords', by Eduard of St Petersburg, c.1910. As is usual, a separate tray below the insignia holds the ribbon to be worn with the Neck Badge.

(Right) An example of a box of issue. As usual, it carries the name and grade of the Order on the lid – in this case the Russian Order of St Anne, Second Class, 'with swords'.

THE ORDERS

THE Orders listed below are the main examples instituted before 1945. Many have become obsolete as the result of political or historical change and some have simply faded into obscurity. Many others – and some of ancient foundation – continue to be conferred by the countries named.

They are listed in their order of precedence – that is, not in date order of foundation, but in the sequence adopted by the state to reflect their status in relation to each other. This is the order in which they would be worn by a recipient who has more than one award.

The Orders are listed by the English translations of their names and are generally referred to by their English names. However, the form of the name in the language of its own country is included, if possible, when each Order is discussed in the text.

Note: in addition to the Orders listed, which are *official* awards conferred by the head of state, there existed throughout Europe from the early Middle Ages independent societies that issued their own Orders and Decorations, usually worn only on formal occasions associated with the society's ceremonies. Such 'Corporations of Knighthood' were common in France and Spain, for example. Orders might also be conferred by minor noble families or even by town guilds.

There are also a number of 'ephemeral' and 'international' Orders, privately produced by individuals, charitable institutions or societies. They carry little international standing and their insignia are rarely seen.

All these unofficial awards are beyond the scope of the present book.

The dates after an award indicate its year of foundation or significant refoundation.

ALBANIA

Formerly part of the Roman and Byzantine empires, the Balkan state of Albania was under Turkish rule from 1478 to 1912, when it gained independence following the Balkan Wars. A kingdom from 1913 to 1939 and occupied by the Italians during the Second World War, it became a communist republic in 1946. After the Balkan civil wars of the late twentieth century, it has emerged as a new republic.

The Order of the Black Eagle, 1914
The Order of Skanderberg, first type 1925, second type 1941
The Order of Loyalty or *Fidelity*, 1926

Albanian Orders are very attractive (the best being produced by leading jewellers in Italy) but rarely seen.

The *Order of the Black Eagle,* established in eight classes by the reigning prince, William of Wied, in March 1914, rewarded military or civil service. The *Order of Skanderberg* (*Urdheri i Skenderbeut*), named after the Albanian hero George Skanderberg (1403–68), was instituted by King Zog in 1925; it had five classes and was conferred for civil and military merit. A slightly different version was created in Albania under Italian occupation, 1941–45, but the 'official' type continued to be awarded by the royal government in exile. The *Order of Loyalty* was effectively a Royal Family Order, established by King Zog in January 1926 for services to the Royal Family. There were five classes.

Albania: Order of Skanderberg. Pre-1940 Neck Badge of the Third Class in silver-gilt and enamel by Giardino of Rome. Those issued under Italian occupation from 1940 to 1944 are of slightly different design.

ANDORRA

This tiny Catalan state, lying between Spain and France in the eastern Pyrenees, was by tradition granted independence by Charlemagne in the eighth century. A principality since 1278, it has no system of Orders.

AUSTRIA

The Duchy of Austria, within the Holy Roman Empire until 1806, became the centre of the great Austrian Empire (known after 1867 as the 'Dual Monarchy' of Austria-Hungary) and one of the great powers of modern Europe under the Hapsburgs. Following her defeat in the First World War and the fragmentation of her empire, Austria was reduced to a small republic. Absorbed into the Nazi Third Reich in 1938, she was restored as a federal republic in 1945.

The Order of St Anthony of Hainault, 1382
The Order of St George, 1273?, 1290, 1470
The Order of the Golden Fleece, 1430 (Burgundy), 1721 (separate
    Austrian branch)
The Military Order of Maria Theresa, 1757–1918
The Royal Hungarian Order of St Stephen, 1764
The Order of Leopold, 1808
The Order of the Iron Crown, 1805–1918
The Order of Francis Joseph I, 1849–1916

(Left) Austria: Order of the Golden Fleece. The Austrian version bears as part of its suspension the motto of the Order (which was that of the House of Burgundy), *Pretium labore non vile* ('The reward of labour is not inconsiderable'), where the Spanish version does not.

(Right) Austria: Order of St Stephen. Sash Badge in gold and enamel of the Grand Cross (i.e. First Class), by Rothe of Vienna. The Order's motto is *Publicum meritorum praemium* ('A public reward of merit').

The Order of the Military Foundation of Elizabeth Theresa, 1750, 1771
The Order of the Starry Cross, 1668–1918
The Order of the Slaves of Virtue, 1662
The Order of St Elizabeth, 1898–1918
The Cross of Military Merit, 1849–1918 (Decoration), 1914–18 (Order)
The Decoration of Honour for Merit to the Austrian Republic, 1922, 1952
The Red Cross Badge of Honour, 1922

Austria's highest Order – one of the most prestigious in Europe – was the *Order of the Golden Fleece* (*Orden von goldenen Vliess*). Founded as a Burgundian award (q.v.) in 1430, it descended in the Hapsburg monarchies of Austria and Spain and was awarded by both countries. It was usually conferred only upon reigning monarchs or on the highest ranks of the nobility; in Austria it was granted only to Catholics, whereas the Spanish version could also be conferred on Protestants. In Austria, the Order was limited to fifty-one members, who were exempted from all taxation and outranked all nobility except royal princes. The Badge of the Austrian version was the same as the Spanish, except that it bears the motto of the Order, *Pretium labore non vile* ('The reward of labour is not inconsiderable').

The *Military Order of Maria Theresa* (*Maria Theresia-Orden*), founded in two classes by the Empress in May 1757, was purely a reward for outstanding leadership or bravery in war. Extended to three classes in 1765, its Grand Cross was conferred only on army commanders for fighting successful campaigns or battles, its Commander's Cross was awarded to senior officers and its Knight's Cross to other officers for conspicuous gallantry.

The *Royal Hungarian Order of St Stephen* (*Königlich Unharischer Orden des Heiligen Stephan*), founded by Empress Maria Theresa in May 1764, was named after Hungary's patron saint, King Stephan I (997–1038), and rewarded exceptional civilian service to the crown or state of Hungary. Apart from the Sovereign as Grand Master, there were only one hundred members and until 1884 recipients of any of its three classes were exempt from state taxation.

Emperor Francis I of Austria established the *Order of Leopold* (*Leopoldsorden*) in January 1808, in memory of his father, Leopold II. Ranking below the Order of St Stephen, its three (later four) classes served to reward military or civil merit.

The *Order of the Iron Crown* (*Orden der eisernen Krone*) 'of Lombardy' was originally a French award (q.v.), instituted by Napoleon in Milan in 1805 to reward his Italian subjects, principally within Lombardy. After Napoleon's fall and the establishment of Austrian control in the province, the Order was re-established by Francis I in 1816. In three classes, it was restricted to one hundred members and served to reward military or civil service, mainly in Austrian Italy.

On the first anniversary of his accession in 1849, the Emperor founded the *Order of Francis Joseph I* (*Franz Josephs-Orden*). In five classes, it could be

(Left) Austria: Order of Leopold. Breast Star of the First Class (Grand Cross), by Rothe of Vienna. It bears the Order's motto, *Integritati et merito* ('For integrity and merit').

(Right) Austria: Order of the Iron Crown 'of Lombardy'. Neck Badge in silver-gilt and enamel. On the refoundation of the Order in 1816, the design was remodelled (see previous French-Italian type on page 35) without the eagle suspension or the motto borne on the French version, and it now carried the 'F' monogram of Francis I in the central shield.

(Left) Austria: Order of Francis Joseph I. First Class (Grand Commander) Breast Star in silver, gold and enamel, by Resch of Vienna. As in many other European Orders, the Star carries the Badge of the Order as its central device.

(Right) Austria: The Order of the Starry Cross in gold and enamel, by Rothe of Vienna.

awarded for special service in almost any field, but it was bestowed particularly on Austrian diplomats and could be conferred on foreigners.

The *Order of the Military Foundation of Elizabeth Theresa (Elisabeth-Theresien-Orden)*, founded under the will of Empress Elizabeth in 1750, was an unusual award. It was conferred on high-ranking military officers of the Empire, regardless of nationality or religion, who had been so severely wounded or injured 'in action' that they could no longer serve or even maintain themselves. Limited to only twenty-one knights, it was in many respects a 'distinguished service' reward and carried high pensions, at three grades, though the Badges of the Order were identical in each case. It was re-established by Maria Theresa in 1771 with amendments to its pensions and allowances.

The attractively named *Order of the Starry Cross (Der hechadelige Sternkreuz-Orden)* was founded by Empress Eleonore in 1668 and comprised just one class, awarded only to Roman Catholic ladies of noble birth, essentially to reward charitable work. It had its origins in unusual circumstances. Following a fire at the royal castle in Vienna in February 1668, the Empress was distressed by the apparent destruction of a valued family heirloom, set with a piece of the True Cross. When it was unexpectedly found undamaged a few days later, the Empress founded the Order in honour of its safe recovery.

Another award restricted to women was the *Order of St Elizabeth*

Austria: Order of St Elizabeth. Breast Badge of the Second Class, worn, as usual with awards to women, from a ribbon bow. The delicate design features a profile of the saint on a cross flory, with roses between the arms.

(*Elisabeth-Orden*), established by Franz Joseph in 1898. In three classes, it was conferred for especially meritorious service to the state.

After the collapse of the Austro-Hungarian Empire in 1918, the Empire was fragmented and Austria became a separate republic. A new Order, the *Decoration of Honour for Merit to the Austrian Republic (Ehrenzeichen für Verdienste)*, was established in November 1922. A complicated award, it technically had seven classes and three lower-tier medals, but as generally awarded it had only six classes. It could be conferred upon Austrian citizens or foreigners for outstanding service to the republic, civil or military.

BELGIUM

Belgium is a modern creation as a nation state. A Burgundian territory in the Middle Ages, and under Spanish rule from the early sixteenth century until 1714, it then passed to the Austrian Empire. After French occupation between 1795 and 1815, the Treaty of Vienna established the Kingdom of the Netherlands (modern Holland and Belgium) under Dutch rule. This union was not popular and in July 1830 the Belgians rose in revolt, creating an independent, neutral Kingdom of Belgium. It was to defend this neutrality that Britain went to war with Germany in 1914.

Belgian Orders and awards – especially the Order of the Crown and the Orders of Leopold – are frequently seen in British medal groups, as a result of alliances in both world wars.

The Order of Leopold or *Leopold I*, 1832
The Order of the Crown, 1897
The Order of Leopold II, 1900
The Order of the African Star, 1888–1960
The Royal Order of the Lion, 1891–1960

The Order of Leopold (*Ordre de Léopold / Leopoldsorde*), Belgium's principal award, was established in July 1832 by her first king, Leopold I. Originally a military reward for gallantry or long service open to all ranks, it is now also conferred for outstanding service to the Crown, civil or military, and may be awarded to foreigners. It has five classes.

The following Orders, all in five classes, were originally established for service in Belgium's huge African territory, the Belgian Congo, after 1881 but were absorbed into the general Belgian system of honours in 1908. The *Order of the African Star* (*Ordre de l'Étoile Africaine / Ordre van de Afrikaanse Stern*) (December 1888) and the *Royal Order of the Lion* (*Ordre Royal du Lion / Kohinklijke Ordre van de Leeuw*) (April 1891) remained principally as rewards for African and colonial service. The former was conferred for significant services to the development of the Congo and 'to African civilisation', whilst the latter was

(Right) Belgium: Order of Leopold I. Sash Badge of the Grand Cross (First Class), in gold and enamel. Its crossed-sword suspension indicates an award in the military division of the Order, whose motto is *La Union fait la force* ('Unity creates strength').

(Far right) Belgium: Royal Order of the Lion. Commander's Neck Badge in silver-gilt and enamel, c.1920.

frequently awarded to African chiefs and local leaders. Both had lower-tier awards in the form of Medals in gold, silver or bronze, and both became obsolete in 1960 when the Congo became independent.

The *Order of the Crown* (*Ordre de la Couronne/Kroonorde*), founded by Leopold II in 1897, is conferred especially for service in the arts, science, literature, commerce and industry. Associated as lower-tier awards are sets of Palms (in gold or silver) and a Medal in gold, silver or bronze. The *Order of Leopold II* (*Ordre de Léopold II/Ordre van Leopold II*) (1900) was originally conferred for personal service to the King but has become the principal award to Belgian diplomats and civil servants for long and/or distinguished service and was also conferred for war service. Military personnel who were mentioned in dispatches in the First World War wore a palm-leaf emblem on the ribbon with 'A' (for King Albert) in the centre; for the Second World War, the palm bore 'L' (for King Leopold). There is also a lower-tier Medal of the Order.

Belgium: Order of the African Star. Commander's Neck Badge. One of a series of Orders originally intended for award in Belgium's African colonies, it was later (1908) extended to general use.

BOHEMIA

The central European state of Bohemia, an important medieval kingdom in its own right, was part of the Austrian Hapsburg dominions between 1526 and 1918. Following the collapse of the Austrian Empire, Bohemia became part of the new Republic of Czechoslovakia in 1919. A Nazi 'protectorate' between 1940 and 1945, it now forms part of the new Czech Republic.

> *The Order of the Knights Hospitallers with the Red Star*, 1217
> *The Hunting Order of St Hubert*, 1695
> *The Order of the Eagle with the Cross*, 1732
> *The Cross for the Bohemian Nobility*, 1814
> *The Order of the Christian Knights*, 1618

The *Hunting Order of St Hubert* (established in 1695 and named after the patron saint of hunting) and the *Order of the Eagle with the Cross* (1732) were both founded, though nearly forty years apart, by the distinguished Bohemian scholar and writer Count Frantisek Sporck.

BULGARIA

The Balkan state of Bulgaria, established in the seventh century, became part of the Byzantine Empire. A major Balkan power in the early Middle Ages, it fell under Turkish rule in 1396. Granted the status of Principality under Turkish suzerainty in 1878 (after the Congress of Berlin), it achieved independence as a kingdom in 1908, was a German ally in both world wars and became a communist 'People's Republic' in 1946. It emerged as a new republic in 1990.

In design, Bulgarian Orders show the influence of other European states, especially Austria and Russia, where many of the best-quality Bulgarian awards were made. Their use of the Cyrillic alphabet also heightens their Russian appearance.

The Order of Saints Cyril and Methodius, 1909–44
The Order of St Alexander, 1878, 1908–44
The Royal Military Order for Bravery in War, 1879, 1908–44
The National Order for Civil Merit, 1891–1944
The National Order for Military Merit, 1900–44
The Order of the Red Cross, 1900, 1908–44

The *Order of Saints Cyril and Methodius* is Bulgaria's highest award, established by King Ferdinand in 1909 immediately after independence and the only royal Order retained after the establishment of the communist regime and into the present day. Named after the ninth-century saints who created, among other things, the Cyrillic alphabet, it has only one class and is conferred on heads of state and the highest-ranking Bulgarian and foreign dignitaries.

(Right) Bulgaria: Order of St Alexander. Neck Badge, second type. This has crossed swords through the piece, denoting a military or war-service award.

(Far right) Bulgaria: National Order for Military Merit. Sash Badge of the First Class. This example is a wartime award of c.1916, in silver-gilt and enamel.

The *Order of St Alexander*, founded by Prince Alexander in August 1878 and named in honour of St Alexander Nevsky, could be awarded for gallantry in action (in which case crossed swords were incorporated into the design) or for outstanding service to the throne. It had six classes.

On his accession as king in 1879, Prince Alexander founded the *Royal Military Order* for war service or bravery in battle. The *National Order for Civil Merit*, established in 1891, was an award for exceptional service to the throne and state; a Military Division was added to it in May 1900. Both had seven classes.

With the exception of the Order of Saints Cyril and Methodius, all the above became obsolete on the formation of the communist republic in 1946.

BURGUNDY

The Duchy of Burgundy, with extensive but scattered lands in eastern France and the Low Countries, was a major state in medieval Europe. Its separate existence effectively ended in the late fifteenth century when its heartland was absorbed into the kingdom of France.

The Order of St George, 1400
The Order of the Golden Fleece, 1430

The most significant Burgundian Order, especially in terms of its later descent, was the *Order of the Golden Fleece* (*L'Ordre de la Toison d'Or*). Instituted

(Left) Bulgaria: Order of Saints Cyril and Methodius. Part of the Collar or Chain of the Grand Cross. It has twenty-five oval plaques charged alternately with fleur-de-lis and crowned lions.

(Right) Burgundy: Order of the Golden Fleece. The Neck Badge shown, essentially the same as the ancient types, is a later version, as worn by recipients of the Spanish version of the Order.

on 10th January 1430, the wedding day of Duke Philip 'the Good' to Isabella of Portugal, it originally comprised only twenty-four Knights. Its title apparently alludes both to the Greek legend of Jason and to the wealth produced in the Low Countries by the wool trade. By descent, the Order passed to both the Spanish and the Austrian Hapsburgs and was conferred by both branches, becoming in 1721 an official award in both empires. In all forms, it was very highly regarded and conferred only on persons of the highest social rank or for exceptional service. (See also Spain and Austria.)

BYZANTINE EMPIRE

The eastern Roman Empire, based on Constantinople (now Istanbul), survived as the Empire of Byzantium until gradually overwhelmed by the Turks; Constantinople itself fell in 1453. The Empire appears to have established its own Orders, about which little is known. One was the *Order of St Samson*, speculatively dated to *c.*1308.

COURLAND

The Duchy of Courland on the Baltic was ruled in the Middle Ages by the Teutonic Order and later by Poland but came under Russian control in 1795. Following the collapse of the Russian Empire, the area became part of the new state of Latvia in 1918.

It had only one Order, the *Order of Merit* (*L'Ordre de la Reconnaissance*), established in 1710 for distinguished service to the state. Examples are rare.

CROATIA

An independent state from 925 to 1102, Croatia was later ruled by Hungary and the Austro-Hungarian Empire and in 1918 became part of the new Yugoslavia. Croatia had no Orders until the Second World War, when, as a puppet state of the Italian and Nazi regimes, it established its own awards. None survived the end of the war and, as they were sparingly conferred, they are now rare, though modern copies exist.

In 1991 Croatia again became independent following the break-up of Yugoslavia.

> *The Order of the Crown of King Zvonimir*, 1942
> *The Military Order of the Iron Trefoil*, 1941
> *The Order of Merit*, 1941–42

The *Order of the Crown of King Zvonimir* (*Orden Kralja Zvonimira*), named after an ancient king of Croatia, and the *Order of Merit* (*Red na Zasluge*) (both in five classes) rewarded those who had aided the Nazi administration, and many were conferred upon German officials and officers. The *Military Order of the*

Iron Trefoil (Mlitär Orden vom Eisernen Dreiblatt) was essentially a gallantry award, in four classes, given to Croatian and Axis personnel for bravery in battle.

CZECHOSLOVAKIA

The central European areas of Bohemia, Moravia and Slovakia, inhabited by the Czechs and Slovaks, were part of the Austrian Empire until its defeat in the First World War, when the Treaty of St Germain (1919) created the Republic of Czechoslovakia. Under German rule between 1939 and 1944, it became a communist 'People's Republic' in 1948 and, like other communist regimes, produced a large range of Orders and awards. In 1992, following the break-up of the Soviet bloc, the country divided to become the Czech Republic and Slovakia.

Czechoslovakian Orders make good use of historic symbols and references to the Bohemian monarchy and heroes of the past.

> The Order for Freedom, 1918
> The Order of the Falcon of Stefanik, 1918–19
> The Order of the White Lion, 1922, 1961
> The Order of Charles IV (or Diploma Badge of King Charles IV), 1936, 1945
> The Order of St Lazarus, 1937
> The Military Order of the White Lion 'for Victory', 1945

The *Order of the Falcon of Stefanik,* founded in November 1918 by the Provisional Government in Paris, was first conferred on members of the

(Left) Croatia: Order of the Crown of King Zvonimir. The Breast Badge of the Second Class, with wreath of oak leaves indicating an award for military or war service.

(Right) Croatia: Order of Merit. Breast Star, First Class; version for Christians. In some Balkan countries and in Russia, there were variations in the design of awards for Christians and non-Christians, since some recipients would not be Christian. This usually involved replacing a cross or saint's image in the design with another motif.

 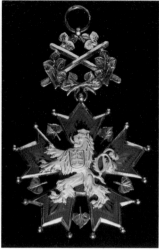 

(Left)
Czechoslovakia:
Order of the
Falcon. Knight's
Breast Badge (the
only grade ever
conferred) of this
rare order.

(Centre)
Czechoslovakia:
Order of the
White Lion. Sash
Badge of the First
Class.

(Right)
Czechoslovakia:
Military Order of
the White Lion 'for
Victory'. Breast
Badge.

Czech Legion serving in Siberia during the Russian Civil War. Planned to be in five grades, only the lowest – Knight – was ever produced, the first ones being made in Tokyo. In 1919 all Orders were abolished as undemocratic but when in 1922 an honours system was re-established the Order of the Falcon was replaced by the *Order of the White Lion* (*Ceskoslovensky rad bileho lva*) as the first new creation. Established in December 1922, this was essentially for foreigners who rendered significant military or civil service to the state. Its five classes were reduced to three in 1961 and it is still awarded. Not to be confused with this is the *Military Order of the White Lion 'for Victory'* (*Ceskoslovensky rad bileho lva 'Za Vitezstvi'*), founded in February 1945 with three classes and two lower-tier medals. It is Czechoslovakia's highest purely military honour and outranks the Order of the White Lion. It may be awarded to Czechs and foreigners for military service or for gallantry in battle.

The *Order of Charles IV*, with its striking portrait of the Emperor (1346–78), was established in 1936 in seven classes for civil and military service.

DENMARK

A kingdom since the tenth century, Denmark was one of the foremost powers of northern Europe in the Middle Ages and once part of the triple kingdom of Norway, Denmark and Sweden. She was re-established as a separate kingdom in 1815 after the Napoleonic Wars.

Since most Danish insignia have to be returned on the death of the holder (with some exceptions for foreign recipients), some official insignia are rarely seen on the market, but privately purchased types do occur.

The Order of the Elephant, 1462?, 1580, 1693
The Order of Dannebrog, 1219?, 1671, 1808, 1842, 1952
The Order of Perfect Unity, 1732
The Order of Sophia Magdalene, 1732
The Order of Matilda, 1771
The Order of Christian VII, 1774

The Danes date their present system of Orders – they now confer only two – to 1693 and the refounding of the *Order of the Elephant* (*Elefantordenen*). Denmark's senior Order, highly regarded and rarely conferred, perhaps dates to as early as 1462 or 1464. It certainly existed by 1508 but it lapsed until 1580, following the Reformation, and it was reintroduced by Christian V in 1693. It was intended to be the equal of the English Order of the Garter and the Hapsburg Golden Fleece and is conferred only for exceptional service. Apart from the Sovereign and his sons, it is limited to thirty members. Notable foreign recipients have been General Eisenhower and Sir Winston Churchill. It has only one class, Knight, and the insignia comprise a Collar with Collar Badge, a Sash with Sash Badge and a Breast Star.

The other major Danish foundation is the *Order of Dannebrog* (*Dannebrogordenen*) or the 'Flag of the Danes'. By tradition, it was established in 1219 by Waldemar II after his victory of Reval, where the miraculous appearance of a red banner with a white cross in the sky is said to have

(Left) Denmark: Order of the Elephant. An early-nineteenth-century Sash Badge of the First Class. As in this example, these are often found as privately commissioned pieces, decorated with pastes or jewels, so that there is considerable variety in their appearance.

(Right) Denmark: Order of Dannebrog. Breast Badge of a Knight, in gold and enamel, worn on a ladies' bow. As is usual with the Dannebrog, the reigning monarch's cipher (here that of Margaret II) is carried between the cross and the crown.

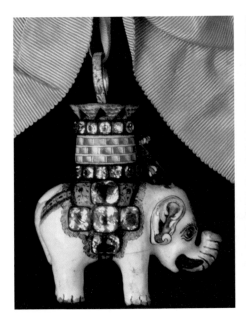

spurred his men on to victory. It was renewed by Christian V in October 1671 and is one of the oldest and most respected Orders in Europe. Originally comprising only fifty Knights, the Order was amended by Frederick VI in 1808 and opened to all citizens and to foreigners regardless of rank for military or civil achievements. In three classes (and two grades) from the rare Grand Commander's Cross, it bears the cipher of Christian V on the obverse and, on the reverse, the dates of its founding and re-establishment – 1219, 1671 and 1808. There is effectively a seventh class in the form of the *Badge of Honour of the Dannebrog*. All insignia are returnable on the death of the holder.

(Left) Ephemeral: 'Order of St Catherine of Mount Sinai'. Breast Star. This 'Order' was founded in 1891 by Guy de Lusignan, who modestly styled himself 'Royal Prince of Jerusalem, Cyprus and Armenia'.

(Right) Estonia: Cross of Liberty. The attractively understated Badge of the Second Grade of the Third Class in dulled silver, blue enamel and gold.

EPHEMERAL OR INTERNATIONAL ORDERS

Over generations, large numbers of unofficial Orders (known as ephemeral, international or fantasy Orders) have been established, many with their own insignia. Most were founded by self-promoting individuals or societies, and membership and insignia could simply be purchased for a donation to funds. Although they have no international standing, some are well produced and they have their own dedicated collectors.

Examples are the French *Order of the Crown of Thorns*, the Greek *Order of St Dennis of Zante*, the French *Royal Order of St Catherine of Mount Sinai* and the Italian *Military Order of St Mary of Bethlehem*, along with many others.

ESTONIA

In the Middle Ages the Baltic coastal province of Estonia was ruled by the Teutonic Knights and later by Poland. It passed to Sweden by 1629 and to Russia in 1721. The region broke away from Russia in 1918 and became an independent republic. Reincorporated into Russia (the Soviet Union) in 1940, it remained under Soviet control until the collapse of the USSR in 1990 and is now an independent republic.

The Order of the White Star, 1928–40
The Order of the Cross of Liberty, 1919–40
The Order of the Cross with the Eagle, 1928–40
The Estonian Red Cross Order of Merit, 1919–40

Since an independent Estonia emerged only in 1918 and was absorbed into the USSR in 1940, its former Orders were short-lived and are rare. Its senior award was the *Order of the White Star*, established in 1928 in eight classes, to reward outstanding civil or military service and it could be conferred on foreigners. The *Order of the Cross of Liberty* was Estonia's first award, founded in three classes in February 1919, initially for meritorious service in the war against Bolshevik Russia in 1917–18, while the *Order of the Cross with the Eagle,* founded in 1928 in eight classes, was awarded for services to national defence.

FINLAND

From the twelfth century Finland was under Swedish rule, eventually as a semi-autonomous Grand Duchy. After 1721 Finland increasingly came under Russian influence and in 1809, during the Napoleonic Wars, was granted to Russia, whose Tsar became Grand Duke. It remained part of the Russian Empire until its collapse in 1917. Up to then, Russian Orders were awarded in Finland but when it became independent these were abolished and Finland instituted its own awards.

Finnish Orders are very distinctive in design and usually of high-quality manufacture.

The Order of the Cross of Liberty or *Order of Freedom*, 1918, 1939, 1941
The Mannerheim Cross of the Order of Liberty, 1940
The Order of the White Rose, 1919
The Order of the Finnish Lion, 1942

The *Order of the Cross of Liberty* (*Vapaudenristen Ritarikunta*) was established in March 1918 as the republic's first Order. Initially to reward service in the war of independence from Russia, it was revised between 1939 and 1944 during

Finland: Cross of Liberty. Breast Badge, by Tillander of Helsinki. This is an award in the Military Division of the Order, indicated by the unusual suspension (sometimes worn as a ribbon emblem), taken from the arms of the province of Karelia. Finland's use of the swastika device in some of its awards is not linked in any way with the Nazi emblem.

29

(Right) Finland:
Order of the
Finnish Lion.
Fourth Class
Breast Badge, by
Tillander of
Helsinki, in silver-
gilt and enamel.

(Left) Finland:
Order of the
White Rose. The
attractive Sash
Badge (top) and
Breast Star of the
First Class, in
silver-gilt, silver
and enamel, by
Tillander of
Helsinki, c.1924.

the second war against Russia. It has six classes and is conferred for
exceptional service to the state but since 1960 has not been awarded as a
civil decoration. It is a complicated award, with over forty combinations of
ribbon emblem (diamonds, oak leaves, swords) or enamel colour and date
variations (1918, 1939, 1941 or undated), according to service or class of
award. Military Badges are distinguished by a ribbon emblem, taken from
the arms of the province of Karelia, in the form of a wreath of oak leaves
from which extend two arms, in armour, holding swords.

The *Mannerheim Cross* was created in December 1940 for gallantry in action
(see medal group illustration on page 10). A unique First Class was conferred
on its namesake, Field Marshal Baron von Mannerheim, the Finnish Regent
who led her forces against Russia in 1918 and again commanded her armies in
the Second World War. Only two of the Second Class Neck Badges and about
two hundred of the Third Class Breast Badges were conferred. It was similar in
design to the Order of the Cross of Liberty, except that its enamel was black.

The most frequently seen Finnish award, often conferred on foreigners,
is the *Order of the White Rose* (*Suomen Valkoisen Ruusan Ritarikunta*), established

in January 1919 as a reward for service to the state, civil or military. It has six classes and two associated medals as lower-tier awards – the silver *Badge of the White Rose* (conferred only on women) and the *Medal of the White Rose*, which itself has three grades.

The *Order of the Finnish Lion* (*Suomen Leijonen Ritarikunta*) was founded in September 1942 in five classes and again rewards service to the state, military or civil, and may be conferred on foreigners. Associated with it is the *Pro Finlandia Medal*, awarded to prominent artists and writers, Finnish or foreign.

FRANCE

The kingdom of France was one of the great powers of Europe but the French Revolution of 1789 destroyed the *ancien régime* of the Bourbon monarchy and created a new republic. In the nineteenth century France (as republic, monarchy or empire) again became a major power and the centre of a world empire. Most of the pre-Revolutionary awards were abolished between 1789 and 1830 but France, re-established as a republic in 1871, still produced an extensive range of Orders, which included colonial types and a large number for service in all sorts of professions. Few areas of French life were without their own system of Orders and Medals, examples being the *Order for Social Service* (1936–63), the *Order of Maritime Merit* (1930–63), the *Order of Public Health* (1938–63), the *Order of Merit in Commerce* (1939–63) and others. The French honours system was overhauled in 1963 and the number of official and 'professional' Orders and Decorations was greatly reduced.

Since France was an ally of Great Britain in the Crimea (1854–56) and in two world wars, her Orders and Decorations, especially the Legion of Honour, are frequently seen in British medal groups.

Medieval France also produced many 'Corporations of Knighthood' and similar associations. These are outside the scope of the present book, but include the Order of the Star (1022?), the Order of the Gold Shield (1363), the Order of the Ermine (1463) and many others. Their insignia are rarely seen.

The *Order of the Holy Vial*, 493?
The *Order of St Michael*, 1469–1789, 1816–30
The *Order of the Holy Ghost*, 1578–1792, 1816–30
The *Order of St Lazarus of Jerusalem and Our Lady of Mount Carmel*, 1608, 1816–30
The *Royal and Military Order of St Louis*, 1693–1792 (for Catholics), 1814–30
The *Order of Military Merit*, 1759–91 (for Protestants)
The *Order of St Hubert 'of Lorraine and Bar'*, 1416
The *National Order of France*, 1789

The Order of the Legion of Honour, 1802, 1871
The Order of the Reunion, 1811–15
The Order of the Iron Crown, 1805 (Franco-Italian), 1816 (Austro-Italian)
The Order of the Lily or *Fleur-de-lys*, 1791 (Bourbon family in exile)
The Order of Loyalty, 1816
The Order of Agricultural Merit, 1883–1963
The Order of the Liberation, 1940–45
The Order of Academic Palms, 1808, 1955

Successive French kings created a wide range of Orders, the majority restricted to those of the highest social rank or holding the highest offices in the state or church. All were swept away between 1789 and 1792 by the French Revolution, and examples of pre-Revolutionary insignia are rare. Awards like the *National Order of France* established by the Revolution and those created or revived during the Napoleonic period, like the Order of the Reunion, were short-lived; only a few survived the fall of Napoleon (examples being the Legion of Honour and the Iron Crown). Some of the older Orders were re-established in 1815–16 following the restoration of the Bourbon monarchy (e.g. the Order of St Michael and the Order of the Holy Ghost) but all became obsolete after the revolutions of 1830 or 1848.

The oldest French Order – and perhaps the oldest in Europe if its foundation date is correct – was the *Order of the Holy Vial (Ordre de la Sainte-Umpoule)*, said to have been founded in 493 by Clovis I. It was exclusively an aristocratic award, and little is known about it. An unsuccessful attempt was made to revive this long-neglected Order in the eighteenth century, and insignia from this era are sometimes seen.

The *Order of the Holy Ghost* (or *Holy Spirit*) was established in 1578 by Henry III to celebrate his accession to the thrones of France and Poland. In one class, it was restricted to one hundred Knights, and its holders vowed to defend the Roman Catholic faith. Declared obsolete in 1791, the Order was revived by Louis XVIII at the Restoration in 1815 as the highest French award, ranking with the English Order of the Garter, and was usually conferred only on French and European royalty. It did not survive the Revolution of 1830 and its insignia are rare. (See illustration on page 12.)

The *Order of St Lazarus of Jerusalem and Our Lady of Mount Carmel (Ordre de St Lazare de Jerusalem et de Notre Dame du Mont Carmel)* originated in 1607 as the Order of Our Lady of Mount Carmel, founded by Henry IV to reward civil and military service. It was combined in 1608 with the resurrected Order of St Lazarus, said to have been established in Palestine in 1060. It was a highly exclusive and rarely conferred award, restricted to those of noble blood. Like other early French awards, it was suppressed in 1791 and briefly revived in the period 1816–30. (See illustration on page 8.)

The *Order of St Michael* (*Ordre de St Michel*), founded in one class by Louis XI in 1469, was intended to reward distinguished service to the state generally and in the fields of art and culture in particular. It too was suppressed in 1791 and briefly revived in the period 1816–30.

The *Royal and Military Order of St Louis* (*Ordre Royal et Militaire de St Louis*) was exclusively an award for Catholics, established in 1693 to reward gallantry in action or service to the Crown. In three classes, it suffered the same fate of suppression (in this case as early as 1789) and resurrection in 1816 as other royal Orders. However, it survived the 1830 Revolution and remained in use until the Revolution of 1848 under Louis Philippe.

The *Order of St Hubert 'of Lorraine and Bar'* (*Ordre de St Hubert*) was founded in May 1416 by Louis I, Duke of Bar, to reward members of the nobility who undertook significant charitable work, such as building churches, orphanages or hospitals. The Order, in one class, was suppressed in 1791, and its Restoration re-establishment was brief, it being finally abolished in 1824.

The *Order of Military Merit* was established in 1759 by Louis XV as a meritorious service reward to Protestant officers of the royal army. Most were conferred on the famous Swiss Guard, the royal bodyguard, many of whom died in the defence of the Tuileries Palace in 1792. It was another royal award that lapsed during the Revolution, was revived on the

(Left) France: Order of St Michael. Sash Badge in gold and enamel of this single-class Order. This is a modern production for museums or collectors; original insignia are rare.

(Right) France: Legion of Honour. Original type of Breast Badge from the later part of Napoleon's reign. His image was used again on awards of this Order under Napoleon III (his nephew) but was replaced by a female head symbolising the Republic after 1871.

Restoration and in this case remained in use until the 1848 Revolution.

The ousted Bourbons issued new Orders to supporters of the royal cause while they were in exile. An early example was the *Order of the Lily* (*L'Ordre de la Fleur de Lys*), created in 1791 by the French royal family and awarded to those who aided the Bourbon cause. Its successor was the *Order of Loyalty* (*Ordre de la Fidélité*), instituted by Louis XVIII in 1816 after his restoration as an immediate reward to those who had supported the royal cause during the Revolutionary and Napoleonic period.

Perhaps the best-known French award is the *Order of the Legion of Honour* (*Légion d'Honneur*). Founded by Napoleon as First Consul in May 1802, it was so highly regarded that it survived his fall in 1815. It was remarkably egalitarian in its intention, with no restrictions imposed by class, rank or status. Personal merit was the only criterion – as befitted the original ideals of the French Revolution. Since the Order remained in use after 1815, there are many design variations from reign to reign. Now in five classes, the Legion of Honour continues to be France's highest award for service to the state in all walks of life. Many, especially of the fourth (*Officier*) and fifth (*Chevalier*) classes, were awarded to British officers and soldiers in wars in which Britain was allied to France – the Crimea 1854–56, China 1856–60, and the First and Second World Wars. (There is a large literature on the Legion of Honour; see *Bibliography of Orders and Decorations* by C. P. Mulder and A. A. Purves, Ordenshistorik Selskab, Copenhagen, 1999.)

The *Order of the Reunion* (*Ordre de la Réunion*), established by Napoleon in 1811 to reward those who had rendered significant aid to his cause, did not outlive his fall in 1815. Its two classes were Knight and Commander. An award that did survive him was the *Order of the Iron Crown* (*Ordre de la Couronne de Fer*), established by Napoleon in Milan in 1805 and intended to reward

(Left) France: Legion of Honour. Sash badge of the Grand Cross (First Class), period of the Third Republic. The Badge has remained essentially the same in design since introduced by Napoleon I, with variations of suspension (crown or wreath) and in the central profile (the reigning monarch, or Napoleon I as founder, or a female head symbolic of the Republic after 1871).

(Right) France: Legion of Honour. The rather plain Breast Star, Third Republic period. It bears the motto (carried with crossed Tricolours on the reverse of the actual Badge) *Honneur et patrie* ('Honour and country') and the date of the refoundation of the Order, 1870.

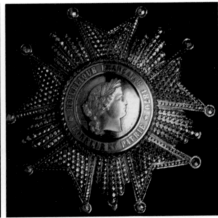

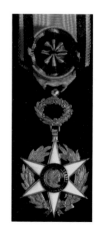

Italian and French citizens for military, cultural or administrative merit, mainly in northern Italy. It had only two classes, Knight and Commander, and its badge in the shape of a crown bore a legend in French or Italian, according to the recipient, pointedly declaring that 'God has given it [the crown] to me; let him beware who touches it'. Following Napoleon's fall, the Order was revived in Lombardy in 1816 by its new ruler, the Austrian Emperor Francis I, and thereafter became an Austrian award (q.v.) for service in her northern Italian provinces.

The *Order of Agricultural Merit*, founded in 1883, was intended, as its name implies, to reward significant work in the realm of agriculture and food production. Somewhat surprisingly, examples of this unmilitary-sounding Order are sometimes seen in British officers' medal groups for 1914–18; these were given for non-combatant work, e.g. in forestry, food or fodder production, veterinary work or remounts, and are perhaps a reminder of the complexity of modern warfare.

The *Order of the Liberation* (*Ordre de la Libération*) was founded by the Free French leader, Charles de Gaulle, in 1940 to reward those who rendered service in the cause of the liberation of France. In one class and strictly a wartime creation, just over one thousand had been conferred before 1946 when the Order was declared obsolete.

(Left) France: Order of the Dragon of Annam. The elaborate Neck Badge of a Commander (i.e. Third Class), made by Bertrand of Paris. An example of a French colonial award for service in France's territories in Indo-China.

(Below) France: Knight's Breast Badge of the Order of the Black Star of Benin. Originally intended to reward service in French West Africa, it was later conferred more generally.

COLONIAL ORDERS

As a world empire, France created Orders to reward service in various specified colonies, especially in Indo-China and Africa. Some were actually created and conferred by local rulers, though the insignia were usually made in France. However, in some cases their award was later extended to cover service in other parts of the empire or in France (e.g. the *Black Star of Benin*).

The principal ones were:

The Order of the Dragon of Annam, 1886–1946
The Order of the Black Star of Benin, 1889–1963
The Royal Cambodian Order, 1864–1946
The Order of the Star of Anjouan, 1874–1963
The Order of Merit of Indo-China, 1900

GERMANY: THE GERMAN STATES

Before *c.*1800, there were over three hundred German states within the Holy Roman Empire, varying from the large and powerful, like Prussia and Bavaria, to small city states hardly larger than the home estates of their ruling

family. Many of their princely families established their own Orders – which means that there are more Orders for the German states than for any other region of Europe. They are a popular collecting field, since most are attractive and of high quality. Some continued to be awarded into the inter-war period, especially for service to the princely family.

Following Napoleon's conquest, the number of states was reduced to about thirty-four but not until the 1860s was a unified Germany created by Prussia, which united the various states between 1864 and 1871 to create the German Empire.

The awards of the German states are beyond the scope of the present work, but see the *Bibliography of Orders and Decorations* by C. P. Mulder and A. A. Purves (Ordenshistorik Selskab, Copenhagen, 1999).

GERMANY: THE GERMAN EMPIRE

After the proclamation of the German Empire in 1871 and the rise of Germany as a European and imperial power, no new 'Imperial German' Orders were created. Those of Prussia (q.v.) were granted as national awards and many German states continued to confer their own Orders, in some cases until well into the inter-war period.

With the defeat of Germany and the creation of the democratic Weimar Republic in 1919, the old Prussian Orders lapsed but the new Republic established no Orders as a matter of egalitarian principle. There were, however, unofficial awards created by nationalist or paramilitary organisations (especially the Freikorps) in the period of domestic upheaval between 1919 and 1923. Only one new Decoration was instituted by the Weimar state: the *Red Cross Decoration of Honour*, established in 1922 for Red Cross and charitable work and renewed in 1939.

A fine Prussian group for 1864–71. It has (from left) the Second Class Iron Cross of 1870; the Order of the Red Eagle, Fourth Class; the Order of the Crown of Prussia, Fourth Class, both 'with swords'; Prussian medals for the Franco-Prussian War, 1870–71, the Austro-Prussian War, 1866, the Danish campaign of 1864; the Russian Order of St Vladimir, Fourth Class; and the 1864 War Cross of the German state of Mecklenburg-Schwerin.

(Left) Prussia: Iron Cross. The First Class of the original foundation of 1813. A plain pin-back cross, based on the ancient badge of the Teutonic Knights, it bears no cipher, no dates and no legend. The awards of this first period (1813–15) are rare.

(Right) Prussia: Iron Cross. Second Class Breast Badge, 1870. It bears the refoundation date '1870' and the monogram of Kaiser William (Wilhelm) I, King of Prussia and first Emperor of the new German *Reich*. There was a non-combatant version of the Iron Cross (e.g. for medical personnel), with the same medal design but reversing the ribbon colours – white with narrow black stripes. The Iron Cross was re-established in 1914 and 1939.

GERMANY: THE THIRD REICH, 1933–45

The Nazi state founded by Adolf Hitler in 1933 and known as the Third Reich (i.e. the third German Empire) put great emphasis on the award of Orders and Decorations, especially for military service, and a new range was rapidly created.

Following her defeat in 1945, Germany was partitioned to form the democratic Federal Republic of West Germany and the communist People's Republic of East Germany (DDR). After the fall of the Berlin Wall, the country was reunified and is now a federal republic.

The Order of Merit of the German Eagle, 1937, 1943–45
The German Order or *Order of Great Germany*, 1942
The German Cross, 1941
The Iron Cross, 1939, 1957
The Blood Order, 1934, 1938–45
The German National Prize for Arts and Science, 1935
The Decoration of Honour of the German Red Cross, 1922, 1939
The Decoration of Honour for Social Welfare, 1939
The Olympic Games Decoration, 1936

The earliest Nazi award was the *Blood Order* – in form just a silver medal – founded to reward the earliest members of the Nazi Party and especially those who were involved in the abortive Munich Beer Hall *putsch* in 1923. The Order was named in memory of the so-called martyrs of the Party who had been killed during the uprising. It was extended in 1938 as an award for service to the party. The opportunity to publicise the Nazi state during the Berlin Olympics of 1936 led to the creation of the *Olympic Games Decoration*, for those who had rendered significant service to the organisation of the showcase games.

The *Order of Merit of the German Eagle* was established in five classes in 1937 and extended to seven in 1943. It was generally conferred only on foreigners, for service to the Nazi state, and had silver and bronze medals as lower-tier awards. It was awarded with or without swords for military or civil service.

Undoubtedly the most famous and often seen Nazi award is the *Iron Cross* (*Das Eisernes Kreuz*). Originally founded as a Prussian military decoration in three classes in 1813, it lapsed until 1870, when it was reinstituted for the Franco-Prussian War, then lapsed again until 1914. During the First World War the Iron Cross was still officially a *Prussian* decoration. The Grand Cross (neck badge) was rarely conferred but the more common pin-back First Class and the Second Class medal were awarded in large numbers. The Decoration was again refounded in September 1939, this time formally as a German (not simply Prussian) award and as an Order. The Nazis added a higher-ranking and highly regarded class, the *Knight's Cross*, worn around the neck, about seven thousand of which were awarded. It could be conferred with a number of emblems for additional or especially outstanding services – Oak Leaves (862 awards), Oak Leaves and Swords (150) and Oak Leaves, Swords and Diamonds (27). There was just one award of the Knight's Cross with Golden Oak Leaves, Swords and Diamonds and a similarly unique Grand Cross, conferred on Reichsmarschall Herman Goering at his own insistence following the fall of France in 1940. In its first and second classes the Iron Cross became the standard reward for gallantry in action. As it was conferred on perhaps as many as five million

Germany, Third Reich: Order of Merit of the German Eagle. Neck Badge of the First Class (1937–43 version). Intended for award only to foreign dignitaries, one Grand Cross was presented by Hitler to Mussolini in Rome in 1937. Lower-tier medals were also associated with this Order.

(Left) Germany, Third Reich: Iron Cross. Neck Badge of the Knight's Cross with Oak Leaves and Swords. The Iron Cross was revived by Hitler as an Order in 1939 and this extra class, with additional emblems such as oak leaves, swords and diamonds, was added as a higher-tier award, essentially for gallantry in action.

(Right) Germany, Third Reich: Order of the German Cross in gold. Shown is the cloth version with gilt central wreath.

recipients, its mass award as the war progressed devalued it in the eyes of its recipients and the quality of materials and manufacture visibly declined. Many dangerous fakes of this award exist in all classes.

In addition to the revived Iron Cross, other Orders were also created. The *German Order* (*Der Deutsche Orden*) is something of a mystery. First conferred in February 1942 and intended for the highest service to the Party, little information on it survives (there are no statutes) and even its formal title is unclear. It may have been intended to become a post-war award and only ten were ever conferred. The *German Cross* (*Das Deutsche Kreuz*), instituted in September 1941, was created to fill the perceived gap between the First Class Iron Cross and the higher Knight's Cross. There were two classes, in gold or silver, the former for bravery in the field and the latter for meritorious military (not civilian) service. Recipients had already to hold the Iron Cross First Class. The pin-back Badge was, unusually, worn on the *right* breast. Some seventeen thousand First Class and nine hundred Second Class awards were made.

All Nazi awards became obsolete in 1945 and the wearing of Nazi emblems was banned. However, in West Germany in 1957 it was decreed that those who had received Orders and medals could wear them in de-Nazified form, with Nazi emblems (e.g. the swastika) erased. Modern versions of these awards thus exist, specially manufactured for veterans, with Nazi symbols removed.

All Nazi Orders and awards have been heavily copied and faked.

GREAT BRITAIN

England developed as a European power after the Norman Conquest of 1066 and increasingly throughout the Middle Ages. She became one of the great European sea powers and trading nations after 1600. The official union of England with Wales (1536), Scotland (1707) and Ireland (1800) created the United Kingdom of Great Britain and Ireland, whilst the Industrial Revolution and imperial expansion led to Britain's becoming the leading industrial and maritime power of the nineteenth century and the centre of a world empire.

Britain has maintained an extensive range of Orders since at least the fourteenth century; its earliest and foremost is the prestigious Order of the Garter (1344/48) and its latest the Order of the British Empire (1917).

The Most Noble Order of the Garter, 1344 or 1348
The Most Ancient and Most Noble Order of the Thistle, 800?, existing by
   1513, revived 1687
The Most Illustrious Order of St Patrick, 1783–1922
The Most Honourable Order of the Bath, 1399; revived 1725
The Order of Merit, 1902
The Most Exalted Order of the Star of India, 1861–1947
The Most Distinguished Order of St Michael and St George, 1818
The Most Eminent Order of the Indian Empire, 1877–1947
The Imperial Order of the Crown of India, 1878–1947
The Royal Victorian Chain, 1902
The Royal Victorian Order, 1896
The Most Excellent Order of the British Empire, 1917
The Order of the Companions of Honour, 1917
The Distinguished Service Order, 1886
The Imperial Service Order, 1902–99
The Indian Order of Merit, 1837–1947
The Order of Burma, 1940–47
The Order of British India, 1837–1947
The Order of St John of Jerusalem, 1888
The Royal Order of Victoria and Albert, 1862–1901 (for ladies)

The three principal British Orders, known as the 'Great Orders', are the Order of the Garter, the Order of the Thistle and the Order of St Patrick.

The *Order of the Garter* was founded by Edward III in 1344 or 1348 during the Hundred Years' War as an aristocratic military fraternity, the Garter perhaps symbolising a bond of unity. It has always been highly exclusive and remains 'in the gift of the monarch', now conferred only for the most

Great Britain: Order of the Garter. Sash Badge known as the 'Lesser George'. Insignia of the Garter rarely appear on the market, as they were to be returned on the death of the recipient. However, many pieces were privately commissioned by their recipients (and therefore retained) and there is a great deal of variety in the quality and manufacture of the badges, etc.

distinguished service to the state over a long period. It has only one class, Knight or Lady (the latter added only in 1987). Its insignia comprise a dark blue Sash, with a Sash Badge depicting St George and the Dragon (known as the 'Lesser George'), a Breast Star and a Collar Chain with pendant Badge (known as the 'George'). An actual Garter, bearing the motto of the Order, *Honi soit qui mal y pense* ('Evil to him who thinks evil of it' — possibly a reference to Edward III's claim to the French crown), is worn above the left knee by men and above the left elbow by ladies. The Order's spiritual home is the Chapel of St George in Windsor Castle, consecrated especially for the Order in 1348.

Scotland's premier Order, the *Order of the Thistle*, may be even older — by legend originating in the eighth or ninth century. It certainly existed by 1513 but is usually dated to its refoundation in 1687. The Order has traditionally been conferred only on the highest ranks of the Scottish nobility or on Scots who have rendered outstanding service to Scotland or Great Britain. In only one class, Knight or Lady (the latter only since 1987), the Order's Chapel is in Holyrood House, Edinburgh. The insignia comprise a dark green Sash with Sash Badge, a Collar with pendant Badge (the Badges depicting the patron saint of Scotland, St Andrew) and a Breast Star which depicts the Thistle, the ancient symbol of Scotland, with the Order's motto, *Nemo me impune lacessit* ('No-one strikes me with impunity').

The third of the Great Orders was the *Order of St Patrick*, founded in 1783, originally to reward the Irish aristocracy for loyalty during the American Revolution and, after the Act of Union in 1800, to reward distinguished Irishmen or service in Ireland. It comprised only twenty-three Knights at any

(Left) Great Britain: Order of the Bath. Neck Badge of a Knight Commander, Civil Division. The Order is unusual in that the insignia are very different for the Civil and Military Divisions. Compare this with the Military KCB (right), for example.

(Right) Great Britain: Order of the Bath. Neck Badge of a Knight Commander, Military Division. The motto of the Order is *Tria juncta in uno* ('Three joined as one'), presumed to be a reference to the Holy Trinity.

time and no ladies were ever admitted. The Order fell into abeyance in 1922 when Ireland was partitioned. As with the other Great Orders, the insignia of this single-class Order comprised a Sash (of sky blue), a Sash Badge featuring the Irish shamrock and red saltire, a Collar with pendant Badge and a Breast Star. Its motto was *Quis separabit?* ('Who shall separate us?').

Another ancient British Order, though ranked below the Great Orders and more frequently conferred, is the *Order of the Bath*. Its unusual title refers to the purification rites associated with the creation of a Knight in the Middle Ages. The Order has existed since at least *c*.1399 but fell into abeyance until revived as a single-class award by George II in 1725, conferred mainly for important military or naval service. As the century progressed, it became another reward in the gift of the monarch for distinguished service to the crown or state in politics and other fields. Its spiritual home is the beautiful Henry VII Chapel in Westminster Abbey. As a result of the French and Napoleonic Wars, the Order was expanded to extend the rewards available to officers of all ranks who had rendered outstanding service. The Order was eventually established in three classes – Knight or Dame Grand Cross (GCB), Knight or Dame Commander (K/DCB) and Companion (CB), the last especially instituted in 1815 to be conferred on officers for recent war service. A single-class Civil Division – unusually with very different insignia – was also created in 1815 and extended to three classes in 1847, to match the military version. The Order is still widely conferred, especially at Companion level, and particularly to long-serving senior officers of the armed forces.

Because of the lack of appropriate rewards for more junior officers on campaign, the *Distinguished Service Order* was created in 1886. It should in fact be regarded as a Decoration and, despite its name, is not a true Order, being in only one class and originally restricted to serving military officers. Since 1993 it has been awarded to all ranks for leadership on campaign and not for gallantry in action.

The acquisition of new territories in the Mediterranean after the Napoleonic Wars led to the creation of the *Order of St Michael and St George*, founded in 1818 by the Prince Regent (later George IV) as a reward for the people of Malta and the Ionian Islands. The Order, in three classes, later became the usual reward for long or distinguished service in the Empire or colonies and to diplomats, colonial administrators, ambassadors, etc, and is still widely conferred.

The last British Order to be created – and by far the most extensively awarded – is the *Order of the British Empire*, instituted in June 1917 by King George V. It was originally intended as a wide-ranging reward for the many people throughout the Empire (hence its title) who had contributed in many professions and fields, military and civil, to the conduct of the First World War. It has more classes than traditional British Orders: Knight or Dame Grand Cross (GBE), Knight or Dame Commander (K/DBE), Commander (CBE), Officer (OBE) and Member (MBE). In addition, it had a lower tier in the form of the Medal of the Order of the British Empire (later known as the British Empire Medal or BEM), though this has been phased out following reforms to the honours system in 1993. The different grades made it possible to recognise achievement and effort at different levels of importance and the

(Left) Great Britain: Distinguished Service Order (DSO). A single-class military award, originally for 'distinguished service', which could mean gallantry, by junior officers on campaign. Following the reforms of the honours system in 1993, it is now awarded only for qualities of leadership but can be conferred on all ranks. The standard reverse is shown; the obverse bears the cipher of the reigning monarch.

(Right) Great Britain: Order of St Michael and St George. Set of insignia of the First Class (Grand Cross or GCMG), showing St George in the centre of the Badge and St Michael on the Breast Star.

(Left) Great Britain: Order of the British Empire. Commander's Neck Badge (CBE) of the Civil Division. This is the first-type Badge, 1918–36, featuring the 'seated Britannia' motif. The ribbon was plain purple, with an added central scarlet stripe for the Military Division.

(Right) Great Britain: Order of the British Empire. Insignia of a Dame Commander (DBE) of the Civil Division, the Badge worn from a bow. This is the second type Badge, after 1936, featuring the conjoined busts of King George V and Queen Mary as founders. The Military Division is signified simply by the addition of a central stripe of pearl grey.

Order is still widely conferred throughout the Commonwealth, especially at its OBE and MBE levels, for service and achievement in all conceivable walks of life.

Three new Orders were specifically linked to Britain's rule in India. After the Indian Mutiny of 1857–59 and the establishment of closer British rule via the India Office and Viceroy, it was considered that greater bonds of loyalty and allegiance should be encouraged. The magnificent *Order of the Star of India* – the most ornate of British awards – was created in 1861 initially to reward Indian princes (the Maharajahs, Rajahs, etc) who had rendered loyal service during the uprising. It later became a high-ranking reward for service within the British Indian Empire and was awarded to administrators, military officers, Indian princes, etc, for distinguished service. It had the usual three classes typical of British Orders – Grand Cross (GCSI), Knight Commander (KCSI) and Companion (CSI), the grade reflecting the importance of the service rewarded. The insignia were beautifully crafted – the Badge surrounded by diamonds and the central cameo of each one a hand-carved profile of Queen Victoria.

The other major Indian award was the *Order of the Indian Empire*, created in 1877 as a result of Queen Victoria's assumption (by the Royal Titles Act of 1876) of the title Empress of India. To avoid offence to any of India's many religions, whose devotees would be potential recipients, the common cross-shaped design was avoided and the Badge took the form of a red enamelled

(Left) Great Britain: Order of the Star of India, Companion's Neck Badge (i.e. post-1917). Each cameo is hand-carved and surrounded by the motto of the order, 'Heaven's light our Guide', picked out in diamonds.

(Right) Great Britain: Order of the Indian Empire. Breast Badge of a Companion (CIE). The Badge was originally larger and had 'I-N-D-I-A' on the petals. It was reduced to a smaller size in 1878. After 1917, this and all other Third Class (Commanders) Insignia were standardised to be worn around the neck, not the breast, as originally established.

rose. The three-class Order was in many ways a lower tier of the Star of India, awarded more freely and for services that were not deemed to merit the Star of India. Nevertheless, the 'Jam Tart' (as it was irreverently called) was highly regarded and was conferred on civil and military recipients, male and female, and of all religions and professions for meritorious service within the Indian Empire.

The rare *Imperial Order of the Crown of India* (1878) was created specifically to reward high-ranking ladies, British and Indian, for achievements in charitable or social work over a long period.

These Indian awards and associated British decorations like the *Indian Order of Merit* (a gallantry award created in 1837), the *Order of British India* (a long-service reward for Indian officers, also created in 1837) and the *Order of Burma* (the Burmese Army equivalent of the OBI, instituted in 1940) became obsolete on Indian independence in 1947.

Several British Orders relate specifically to the Royal Family and royal service. Since 1820, a *Royal Family Order* has been conferred by the reigning monarch exclusively on female members of the Royal Family. The Badge, a miniature portrait of the sovereign surrounded by diamonds, is worn from a bow from the left shoulder. Queen Victoria instituted a personalised type in 1862, the *Royal Order of Victoria and Albert*. In four classes, its first and second classes, with a cameo profile of Victoria and Albert, were conferred only on female members of British and foreign royalty, while the third and fourth classes could be conferred upon high-ranking ladies, often members of the royal household. It ceased to be awarded after the Queen's death in 1901.

The last Order created during the nineteenth century was the *Royal Victorian Order*, founded in 1896 by Queen Victoria. At a time when the honours system was increasingly falling under political influence, the Queen wished to create an Order that would remain in royal control and enable a reward to be given to those who had rendered significant service to the Royal Family. The Order is still awarded for such services and now has five classes – Knight or Dame Grand Cross (GCVO), Knight or Dame Commander (K/DCVO), Commander (CVO), Lieutenant (LVO) and Member (MVO). There is a lower-tier award, the *Medal of the Royal Victorian Order* (RVM), which can be conferred in gilt, silver or bronze and is usually awarded to those below officer rank for services on royal occasions such as state visits and royal funerals, or to the domestic and personal staff of the Royal Family for long or meritorious service (see title page).

The highly exclusive *Royal Victorian Chain* (1902) is a single-class Collar and Badge similar to but quite separate from the Royal Victorian Order, conferred by the monarch on persons of high rank for long and important service (e.g. Archbishops of Canterbury on retirement).

Two awards were created for outstanding achievement. The *Order of Merit* (OM), worn as a single-class Neck Badge, was created by Edward VII in 1902 and is conferred for the most distinguished contributions to art, science, industry, literature, music, etc, and is restricted to twenty-four members, military or civil. Some of the most important figures in modern British culture have received the award – Edward Elgar, Bertrand Russell, T. S. Eliot, Winston Churchill, Lord Kitchener, as well as foreign honorary members, such as Nelson Mandela.

What may be considered as a lower-tier award, the *Order of the Companions of Honour* (CH), was created in 1917 and similarly rewards service 'of national importance' to Britain or the Commonwealth in culture, science, education, industry, etc. The Order, worn as a single-class Neck Badge, is restricted to sixty-five members; a few recipients (including Sir Michael Tippett and Sir Winston Churchill) also held the Order of Merit.

GREECE

Greece – the centre of an ancient civilisation – came under Roman rule after 147 BC and was later part of the Byzantine Empire. Conquered by the Turks after 1450, Greece achieved independence after a war between 1821 and 1829 and was established as a monarchy in 1832. The country was a republic from 1922 to 1935, when the monarchy was restored. After Italian and German occupation in the Second World War, the monarchy was restored again in 1945 but was overthrown in 1973 and Greece again became a republic. All monarchist Orders were declared obsolete in 1973.

Greek awards are very attractive and of high quality, many of them made by leading jewellers in Russia or France.

The Order of the Redeemer or *Order of the Saviour*, 1829–1973
The Order of George I, 1915–24, 1936–73
The Order of the Phoenix, 1926 (republic), 1936–73 (monarchy)
The Order of St George and St Constantine, 1936–73
The Order of St Olga and St Sophia, 1936–73

(Left) Greece: Order of the Redeemer. Sash Badge and Breast Star of the Grand Cross (First Class). Post-1863 (second) type, with a beautifully enamelled image of Christ as the central motif, replacing the profile of Otto I. The legend reads 'The Order of the Redeemer'.

Greece's first and most prestigious award was the *Order of the Redeemer* (*Basilikon tagma toi Soteros*). Founded in July 1829 to reward those who had served in the War of Independence, it was named in gratitude for the salvation of Greece from the Turks. Re-instituted in 1833 by Greece's first king, Otto I, as a general award in five classes, it rewarded exceptional service to Greece and could be conferred on foreigners. Up to 1862 its central medallion bore the effigy of Otto I (see illustration on page 6) but after 1862 it bore a fine enamelled portrait of Christ. Examples are found in British groups for 1915–18 service, when Greece was an Allied power.

The *Order of George I* (*Basilikon tagma toi Georgoiy A*) was established in six classes in January 1915 by King Constantine I and named in honour of his father, who was assassinated in 1913. It rewarded distinguished service in the fields of art, science and public administration or in times of war. Military

Greece: Order of George I. Grand Cross, set by Keladis of Athens. This set is from Greece's period as a kingdom, before 1973, with the royal crown incorporated into the design. The central legend means 'The love of my people [is] my strength'. This is another good example that illustrates how the Breast Star can carry the main design of the Badge of the Order.

awards bore crossed swords through the central design. During the Republic of 1926–35, it was replaced by the new *Order of the Phoenix (Basilikon tagma toi Phoinikos)*, symbolising the rebirth of the republic, in five classes and awarded for similar services. When the monarchy was restored in 1936 both the *Order of George I* and the *Order of the Phoenix* were retained as national awards.

What were essentially two Royal Family Orders were established by the restored monarchy of George II in 1936. The *Order of St George and St Constantine (Basilikon oikogenaiakon tagma ton agion Georgioy kai Konstantinoi)* is reserved for men and at its highest levels for members of the Royal Family only. There were civil and military divisions, each of five classes. Its equivalent award to women only, and again usually of the Royal Family, was the *Order of St Olga and St Sophia (Basilikon oikogenaiakon tagma ton arion Sophias kai Olgas)*, in four civil classes. The lower grades of both Orders could be conferred on commoners or foreign nationals for exceptional service to the Greek royal house.

HOLLAND: SEE THE NETHERLANDS

THE HOLY LAND

As a result of the Crusades between 1095 and 1291, various 'Crusader kingdoms' were established in the Holy Land (Palestine). In imitation of European practices, their leaders instituted a range of Orders, but little is known about them. They ceased to exist following the destruction of the Crusader kingdoms with the fall of the Holy Land to the Turks at the end of the thirteenth century.

Information about their origins and nature is largely speculative but known examples, most dating to the era of the Third Crusade of 1189–92, are:

The Order of St Cosmas and St Damian or *The Martyrs in Palestine*, 1030?
The Order of St John of Acre, twelfth century?
The Order of Mont Joie, 1180?
The Order of Fortuna, 1190?

HUNGARY

The central European area occupied by the Huns after the fall of the Roman Empire was conquered by the Magyars in 876 and was an independent kingdom from 1001. On the margins of the Holy Roman Empire, it was from 1526 to 1918 part of the Austrian Empire under Hapsburg rule, after 1867 as the 'Dual Monarchy' or Austro-Hungarian Empire. After Austria-Hungary's defeat in the First World War, the Treaty of St Germain created an independent (briefly communist) republic. From 1920 to 1944, Hungary was nominally a kingdom under the regency of the dictator Admiral Horthy and was a German ally in the Second World War. It reverted to a republic in 1946 and became a communist 'People's Republic' in 1949. An anti-Soviet uprising in 1956 was suppressed, but with the fall of the USSR and the break-up of its power bloc Hungary emerged as an independent republic in 1989.

(Below) Hungary: Order of St Stephen. Breast Star in silver-gilt and enamel of the Grand Cross, by Rothe of Vienna.

The Royal Hungarian Order of St Stephen, 1764–1918
The Order of the Golden Spur, 1919

The Hungarian Order of Merit, 1922–44
The Decoration of the Hungarian Red Cross, 1922–44
The Order of Vitez for Bravery, 1921
The Order of the Holy Crown of St Stephen, 1942–44

While Hungary was part of the Austro-Hungarian Empire Austrian imperial Orders were current. A more specific award was the *Royal Hungarian Order of St Stephen* (*Königlich Unharisher Orden des Heiligen Stephan*). Founded by the Empress Maria Theresa in May 1764 as a reward for exceptional service in or to Hungary, it was conferred in three classes and until 1884 recipients were exempt from national taxes. It was named after Hungary's patron saint and early ruler, Stephen I (997–1038), who brought Christianity to the country.

Hungary: Order of Vitez. The pin-back Breast Badge.

The *Order of the Golden Spur* was a rarely conferred and short-lived Order established at the time of Hungary's emergence as a new republic in 1919. There is a Vatican Order with the same title (q.v.).

Under the dictator Admiral Horthy several new awards were introduced, none surviving his fall in 1944. Most were introduced during the Second World War as military rewards and many were conferred on German officers and officials. The *Order of the Holy Crown of St Stephen* had five classes and was conferred for military or civilian service in time of war, especially to foreigners who had served Hungary. The actual Crown of St Stephen depicted on the Badge is the honoured, ancient symbol of Hungary and was restored to the country in 1977, after being in the United States since the end of the Second World War. The *Order of Vitez* (*A Vitezi Rend*), in the form of a pin-back pocket Badge, was specifically a gallantry award, *Vitez* meaning 'warrior' or 'knight'.

As with other post-war communist states, Hungary later produced a range of Orders covering service and achievement in all walks of life.

ICELAND

The remote island of Iceland was first settled in 874 and was from 1262 a possession of the Danish Crown. It became an independent republic in 1944.

The Order of the Icelandic Falcon, 1921

The only Icelandic Order, the *Order of the Icelandic Falcon* (*Hin islenzska falkaorda*), was established on 3rd July 1921 by Christian X of Denmark and Iceland. Retained when Iceland became a republic, it is still awarded. The Order has five classes and may be conferred on citizens or foreigners for outstanding service, military or civil. After 1944, the royal crown was removed from the insignia and the date of the formation of the Republic (17th June 1944) added to the reverse. As all insignia have to be returned on the death of the holder, examples rarely appear on the market.

(Opposite page, right) Iceland: Order of the Icelandic Falcon. Breast Badge of a Knight, second type (republican issue without crown), by Asmundsson of Reykjavik, worn on a lady's bow.

IRELAND

The Republic of Ireland (Eire) was established as a Free State in 1922 and a republic in 1949. It has no system of Orders.

ITALY: THE ITALIAN STATES

Before the *Risorgimento* and unification under the House of Savoy between 1860 and 1871 the Italian peninsula was occupied by a number of independent princely states, city states or republics, examples being Modena, Parma, Tuscany and Genoa. Many are familiar as centres of the Renaissance, such as Venice, Florence and Naples. Since most were ruled by noble families or at times controlled by other powers whose Orders were used, most had their own series of awards. They were generally conferred sparingly, usually on the highest ranks of the nobility, foreign aristocrats, senior officials or senior members of the Catholic Church, and are rare. After unification and the establishment of a national system (based on the awards of the ruling House of Savoy), some state Orders continued to be awarded but these may be considered as little more than 'House Orders' or personal gifts.

The Orders of the Italian states are beyond the scope of this work, but see *Bibliography of Orders and Decorations* by C. P. Mulder and A. A. Purves (Ordenshistorik Selskab, Copenhagen, 1999).

ITALY

The *Risorgimento* led by King Victor Emmanuel II, Count Cavour and Giuseppe Garibaldi brought about the unification of the Italian states between 1866 and 1871 under the leadership of the House of Savoy, the rulers of Piedmont-Sardinia. Many of the existing Orders of the House of Savoy remained in use as national honours after 1871 but a new range of awards was also established. Italy was an Allied power during the First World War (so that examples of its awards, especially the Crown of Italy, are found in British groups) but became a fascist dictatorship with Mussolini as Prime Minister from 1922 to 1943. Italy was liberated from its occupying German forces by the end of 1945 and became a republic in 1946, when most royal Orders became obsolete.

The Order of the Golden Angel or Order of St George, 312?
The Order of the Royal Crown, 802?
The Order of the Annunciation, c.1362, 1518 (Savoy), 1867–1944 (Italy)
The Order of the Lily, 1546
The Order of the Jubilee Brethren, 1233?
The Order of the Iron Crown, 1805–14
The Order of the Necklace, 1360

The Order of St Maurice and St Lazarus, 1572 (Savoy), 1816 (Sardinia),
  1867– 1944 (Italy)
The Order of the Crown of Italy, 1868–1946
The Order of Military Merit (originally the *Military Order of Savoy*), 1815,
  1855 (Savoy), 1867 (Italy), 1947, 1956
The Colonial Order of the Star of Italy, 1911
The Order of Civil Merit, 1831
The Order for Merit for Labour, 1901
The Order of the Roman Eagle, 1942–44

Information on Italy's earliest awards is speculative – few facts are known
about the *Order of the Golden Angel* (said to date to AD 312) and the *Order of
the Royal Crown* (802?).

The most important Order of the House of Savoy was the magnificent
Order of the Annunciation (*Ordine della Sacrata Annunciazione*), founded *c.*1362 as
the Order of the Collar by Amadeus, Count of Savoy (see illustration on page
6). Named in honour of the 'fifteen joys of the Virgin', it had fifteen Knights
and fifteen Chaplains, who said fifteen masses every day. Its original statutes
had fifteen clauses. It ranked with the English Order of the Garter and the
Burgundian/Austrian/Spanish Golden Fleece in status. Having lapsed, it was
re-established in 1518 by Charles III as the Order of the Annunciation and
became a national Order in 1867 after Italian unification under Victor Emmanuel
II. It was conferred only for the most important services, and recipients had to
have already received the Order of St Maurice and St Lazarus. It was generally

Italy: Order of St
Maurice and St
Lazarus. The Neck
Badge and Breast
Star. In these very
attractive and
distinctive badges,
the green Maltese
cross represents St
Lazarus while the
cross botonny
represents St
Maurice.

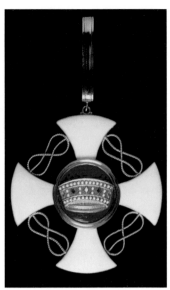

(Left) Italy: Order of the Crown of Italy. The Breast Star carries in the centre the Badge of the Order, with the 'Iron Crown of Lombardy' in enamels, and delicate gold love-knots between the arms of the cross.

(Right) Italy: Order of the Crown of Italy. Second Class Neck Badge.

granted in Italy only to Roman Catholics, but exceptions were made for foreign recipients (like the Duke of Wellington), and it had just one class. Recipients wore both a Breast Star and a Neck Badge, suspended from a collar or chain.

The *Order of St Maurice and St Lazarus* (*Ordine de SS Maurizio e Lazzaro*) was established in 1572 as a military order when the Pope united the ancient Order of St Maurice (founded in 1434 by Amadeus VIII, first Duke of Savoy, 1382–1450) and the lapsed Order of St Lazarus, a brotherhood established in the Holy Land c.1060 (and later extended to France and Naples) to aid lepers. It was adopted in 1600 by Charles Emmanuel I of Savoy, extended in 1816 to the state of Sardinia (under the rule of the House of Savoy) and became an Italian Order in 1867 following Italian unification. In five classes, it was awarded only to Catholics, foreigners included, for meritorious service to the Kingdom of Italy.

The *Order of the Crown of Italy* (*Ordine della Corono d'Italia*) was established by Victor Emmanuel II in February 1868 on his accession as king of a united Italy and in celebration of the unification of the country. A much awarded Order, it had five classes and was conferred on Italians or foreigners for exceptional services to Italy. It is sometimes seen (particularly in its lower grades) in British officers' medal groups, especially for the First World War.

The *Order of Military Merit* was created by Victor Emmanuel I in 1815 as the *Military Order of Savoy* (*Ordine Militare di Savoia*), revived in 1855 when Sardinia was fighting in the Crimean War, and adopted as an Italian national award in 1867. Unusually, it survived the fall of the monarchy and was re-established in 1947. In five classes, it is awarded for exceptional military service or merit and is now known as the *Military Order of Italy*.

In emulation of other powerful European states, notably France and Britain, the new Italian kingdom sought to establish an overseas empire, especially in Africa. The *Colonial Order of the Star of Italy* (*Ordine Coloniale della Stella d'Italia*) was established by Victor Emmanuel III in 1911 at the time of Italian conquests in North Africa and was intended to reward colonial service. It had five classes.

The *Order of Civil Merit* was established as the *Civil Order of Savoy* (*Ordine Civile di Savoia*) in Turin in October 1831 by Charles Albert (1798–1849); he was the first of the kings of Piedmont-Sardinia to strive for Italian unification, in his case fighting Austrian domination. Conferred in only one class, Knight, it was intended to reward distinguished achievement in those professions that were 'not less useful than the army'. A similar civil award in one class was the later *Order for Merit for Labour* (*Ordine al Merito del Lavoro*), established in 1901 to reward service in the fields of labour relations, inventions and industry.

The short-lived *Order of the Roman Eagle* (*Ordine Aquila Romana*) was founded by the King in March 1942 primarily as an award to foreigners for exceptional service. This effectively meant rewarding German military officers and officials. The Order had five classes and two lower-tier medals. With the surrender of Italy in September 1943, the Order remained in use in the German-controlled remnant of fascist Italy but effectively ceased to exist by 1945.

(Left) Italy: Military Order of Savoy. Neck Badge and Breast Star. The attractive Badge, with a cross urdy carrying the white cross emblem of Savoy, has *Al merito militare* ('For military merit') in the centre, while the Star has the refoundation date '1855'.

(Right) Italy: Order of the Roman Eagle. Breast Badge of the Fourth Class (with rosette). The Order was established by the King in 1942 when Italy was a fascist state under Mussolini.

LATVIA

The Baltic region now known as Latvia ('the country of the Letts') was ruled by the Teutonic Knights from the thirteenth century until 1560. As Livonia, it came under Polish influence until 1621, when it was united with Sweden, and in 1710 with Russia. Like its neighbours Estonia and Lithuania (q.v.), it broke away in 1918 with the fall of the Russian Empire. Russia regained control in 1940 and Latvia remained part of the USSR until the collapse of the Soviet bloc. It was re-established as an independent republic in 1991.

Apart from any newly created awards, Latvia's Orders were established during its brief period of independence between the world wars and were sparingly issued. They rarely appear on the market.

> *The Order of the Three Stars*, 1924–40
> *The Order of Lacplesis the Bear Slayer*, 1919–40
> *The Order of Vesthardus*, 1928, 1938–40
> *The Order of the National Guard*, 1928
> *The Red Cross Order*, 1927–40
> *The Order of the Cross of Merit*, 1938–40

The *Order of the Three Stars* (*Triszvaigzhnu Ordenis*) was Latvia's highest award for civil merit and came in five classes. The strangely named *Order of Lacplesis*

(Left) Latvia: Order of the Three Stars. Commander's (i.e. Third Class) Neck Badge. The short-lived republic's highest award, it existed for only sixteen years.

(Right) Latvia: Order of Lacplesis the Bear Slayer. Neck badge of this rare order.

the *Bear Slayer* (*Latczplesha Kara Ordenis-Lacplesis*) was established in November 1919 in three classes as Latvia's highest military decoration, initially for service during the war of independence against the Bolsheviks in 1918–19. It was named after the Latvian mythical hero Lacplesis, who was credited with great strength and courage. The *Order of Vesthardus* (*Viestura Ordenis*), named after a thirteenth-century Latvian king, was awarded in five classes and rewarded outstanding military service.

LIECHTENSTEIN

This small principality on the Swiss-Austrian border, established in 1342, was named Liechtenstein in 1719 after its Austrian ruling family. Although a member of the German Confederation from 1815 to 1866, it did not join the German Empire in 1871 and has been an independent state since 1866.

Liechtenstein: Order of Merit of the Principality – the state's only Order. Commander's (i.e. Third Class) Neck Badge.

The Order of Merit of the Principality, 1937, 1960

Liechtenstein's only Order is the *Order of Merit of the Principality* (*Der fürstliche liechtensteinische Verdienstorden*) established by Prince Franz I in July 1937 and enlarged in 1960. It has eight classes and is awarded to citizens and foreigners for meritorious service to the Principality. Associated with it is a lower-tier *Medal of Merit* in two classes, gold and silver.

LITHUANIA

The Baltic province of Lithuania, established as a Grand Duchy in the thirteenth century, became a large and powerful state by 1420. Thereafter, it came under Polish influence and in 1569 was united with Poland. With the dismemberment of Poland, Lithuania came under Russian rule from 1776 to 1918 and, like its neighbours Estonia and Latvia (q.v.), achieved independence on the fall of the Russian Empire in 1918. Reoccupied by the Russians in 1940, Lithuania remained part of the Soviet bloc until the collapse of the USSR and was re-established as an independent republic in 1990.

Apart from any newly created awards, Lithuania's Orders date from the brief period of independence between the world wars and are rare.

The Order of Grand Duke Gedeminas, 1928–40
The Order of the Cross of Vytis, 1918–40
The Order of Vytautas the Great, 1930–40

The *Order of Grand Duke Gedeminas* (*Ordinas Gedemino*), founded in 1928, rewarded exceptional civilian achievement and was Lithuania's most frequently awarded Order. It was named after the Grand Duke who defeated

(Left) Lithuania: Order of Grand Duke Gedeminas. Neck Badge of the Second Class, c.1928. This very distinctive design features in its centre a stylised representation of the gates of Trakai Castle, the crest of the fourteenth-century hero, Grand Duke Gedeminas.

(Right) Lithuania: Order of Vytautas the Great. Breast Star: as is commonly the case, the central motif – here a crowned Greek cross with 'spade' ends – is essentially the Badge of the Order.

the Russians in 1321 and founded the country's capital, Vilnius, in 1323. The Order, which could be conferred on foreigners, came in five classes. The *Order of the Cross of Vytis* (*Vytis Kryzius*) was Lithuania's highest award for gallantry and military service and was established in November 1918 in three classes. The *Order of Vytautas the Great* (*Ordinas Vytauto Didziojo*) was created in 1930 to commemorate the five-hundredth anniversary of the death of Saint Vytautas, the Grand Duke who brought Christianity to the region and who defeated the Teutonic Knights at Tannenburg in 1410. Conferred for outstanding civil or military service, it was awarded in three classes and could be conferred upon foreigners.

LUXEMBOURG

The County of Luxembourg (or Luxemburg), on the north-eastern French border, emerged in the eleventh century and was named after its principal town. A Duchy from 1354, it passed to Burgundy in 1444, thereafter sharing the descent of other Burgundian territories – Spanish rule from 1555 to 1713, then Austrian to 1795, when it was conquered by the French. It was created a Grand Duchy by the Treaty of Vienna in 1815 and became an independent, neutral state in 1867.

The Order of the Golden Lion of Nassau, 1858, 1906
The Order of the Oaken Crown, 1841
The Order of Adolph of Nassau, 1858, 1890

Luxembourg: Order of the Golden Lion of Nassau. Breast Star. This is a variant version, displaying the profile of Duke Adolph in place of the usual depiction of a golden lion.

The *Order of the Golden Lion of Nassau* (*Ordre du Lion d'Or de la Maison de Nassau*) was established in January 1858 as a Family Order for both the Netherlands and Luxembourg branches of the House of Nassau. Reserved for members of the ducal family or for those of high rank (e.g. generals and archbishops), it has only one class, Knight. The *Order of Adolph of Nassau* (*Ordre du Mérite d'Adolph de Nassau*) was established by Duke Adolph in May 1858 but abolished in 1866 when the Duke's homeland of Nassau was incorporated

(Left) Luxembourg: Order of Adolph of Nassau. Commander's Neck Badge, with crown suspension, in silver-gilt and enamel.

(Right) Luxembourg: Order of the Oaken Crown. Breast Badge of the Fourth Class (Officer). The central motif is a crowned 'W', recalling the Order's founder in 1841, William II, King of the Netherlands and Grand Duke of Luxembourg.

into Prussia. It was reinstated in 1890 when Adolph became Grand Duke of Luxembourg and may be awarded to citizens and foreigners for service to the Duchy or ducal family or for achievement in the arts and sciences. It has both a civil and a military division, each of five classes. Awards for service in the Second World War bore a silver-gilt palm on their ribbon. Associated with this Order as lower-tier awards are the *Medal for Art and Sciences* in gold or silver and the *Medal of Merit* in gold, silver or bronze.

The *Order of the Oaken Crown* (*Ordre de la Couronne de Chêne*) was founded in December 1841 by William II, King of the Netherlands and Grand Duke of Luxembourg. It is awarded for civil or military service to the state or artistic achievement, and all insignia must be returned on the death of the holder. Associated with the Order as a lower-tier award is an eight-sided *Medal of Merit*, in gold, silver or bronze.

MALTA

From the late Middle Ages the strategically placed Mediterranean island of Malta was controlled by the Knights of the Order of the Hospital of St John

(Left) Malta: Order of Malta. Neck Badge (with elaborate trophy of arms suspension). It utilises the familiar white Maltese cross and black ribbon used with the Badges of many of the branches of the Order of St John around the world.

(Right) Prussia: Johanniter Order. Neck Badge of a Knight of Justice. This is a Prussian Protestant version of the Order of St John of Jerusalem, using the familiar Maltese cross and black ribbon of the Order.

of Jerusalem. Founded as a military Order in Jerusalem at the time of the First Crusade, they moved to Rhodes when the Holy Land fell to the Turks in 1291 and after the fall of Rhodes in 1522 were given Malta as their fortress base. The 'Sovereign Order' remained in control of Malta until expelled by Napoleon in 1798. Malta became a British possession in 1815 and an independent republic in 1964.

The Order of St John still exists (based in Rome since 1827) and is nowadays known for its hospital and charitable work. Many other European states, including Great Britain, have their own separate versions.

The Order of Malta, 1113
The Cross of Merit of the Sovereign Military Order of Malta, 1916, 1920
*The Johanniter Order, c.*1550, 1812, 1853

The *Order of Malta* (created by the Catholic Sovereign Military Hospitaller Order of St John of Jerusalem, of Rhodes and of Malta) was originally established in 1113 and is the oldest *continuously awarded* Order in Europe. It has a complicated arrangement of classes, the principal ones being Knights or Dames of Justice, Knights or Dames of Honour and Devotion, and Knights or Dames of Grace. Branches of the Catholic Order established in various European countries often have their own distinctive versions of the Badges.

The *Cross of Merit of the Sovereign Military Order of Malta* was founded by the Order in Austria in 1916 and extended throughout the whole Order in 1920. In five classes (with a Grand Collar for heads of state) it is awarded regardless of creed to those who have rendered outstanding service to the Order of St John.

The *Johanniter Order* was established by the Order of St John in Brandenburg (Prussia). This branch became Lutheran following the Reformation and conferred the Order on Protestant recipients. In three classes, it was later extended to Protestant members of the Order in a number of other European countries (e.g. Sweden, Netherlands, Finland, Hungary).

Great Britain has its own entirely separate version of the Order of St John, which was also established throughout the British Empire and English-speaking world.

MONACO

The independence of Monaco, based around Monte Carlo on the French Mediterranean coast, was first recognised in 1489. Ruled by the Grimaldi family since 968, with only brief breaks in their control, it became a constitutional monarchy in 1911.

The Order of St Charles the Holy, 1858

For nearly a century the *Order of St Charles the Holy* (*Ordre de St Charles*), founded in March 1858 by Prince Charles III, was the Principality's only Order. It may be conferred on foreigners or citizens for services to the state or ruling family and has five classes. Three other Orders were established after 1945: the *Order of Cultural Merit* in 1952, the *Order of the Grimaldi* in 1954 and the *Order of the Crown* in 1960.

MONTENEGRO

The Balkan state of Montenegro ('Black Mountain') on the Adriatic coast has been independent as a principality since the fourteenth century, its independence formally recognised by the Turks in 1878 following the Treaty of Berlin. A monarchy since 1910, it was incorporated into the Serbian-dominated Yugoslavia, created in 1919 (q.v.). Montenegro was communist from 1945 (as part of Yugoslavia) but has emerged as an independent republic following the Balkan Wars of the 1990s, which fragmented Yugoslavia.

The few Montenegrin Orders are very attractive, mostly manufactured in Vienna (before 1918) or in Switzerland.

> The Order of St Peter (or Order of Independence or Order of the Prince of
>   Montenegro), 1852–1919
> The Order of Danilo (or Order of the Tschernagorian Independence),
>   1852–1919
> The Red Cross Order, 1913–19

Montenegro's highest award was the *Order of St Peter*, established by the ruling prince, Danilo I, in 1852. It had only one class and was awarded solely to the Royal Family and to foreign heads of state. It became obsolete in 1919 when Montenegro was absorbed into Yugoslavia and examples are rare.

The *Order of Danilo*, established in four classes by Danilo I in May 1852 to reward outstanding civil or military service, was named in honour of Danilo Petrovic Njegos, founder of the ruling dynasty of Montenegro, who secured the protection of Russia in 1716. It was retained after the assassination of Danilo I in 1860 but like other Montenegrin awards became obsolete in 1919. Examples of this award are occasionally found in British groups for 1914–18 service.

The *Red Cross Order* was granted to those who rendered medical assistance to the army of Montenegro during the Balkan Wars of 1912–13, which resulted in the final removal of Turkish influence in the area. Some were conferred upon British volunteer doctors and nurses, but examples are rare.

Montenegro: Order of Danilo. Commander's Neck Badge. The Cyrillic inscription has the name of the Order around the cipher of Danilo I; the Order's foundation date, '1852–53', is carried in the reverse centre. The Badge of the lowest (Fifth) class is plainer, in black enamel, without crown.

THE NETHERLANDS

Like Belgium (q.v.), the provinces of Holland were part of the Spanish Netherlands in the late Middle Ages and fought a series of wars after 1572 to gain a degree of independence as the Protestant 'United Provinces'. From 1650, Holland became one of the great maritime and trading powers of Europe, creating an extensive overseas empire, especially in the Far East. Holland came under French rule from 1793 to 1814, but the Treaty of Vienna in 1815 united Holland and Belgium as the Kingdom of the Netherlands. Belgium seceded from the Kingdom in 1830, leaving Holland as an independent kingdom under a constitutional monarchy.

> The Grand or Royal Order of the Union, 1806–10
> The Royal Order of Merit, 1806
> The Royal Order of Holland, 1807
> The Military Order of William, 1815
> The Order of the Netherlands Lion, 1815
> The Order of Orange-Nassau, 1892
> The Royal Family Order of the House of Orange, 1905, 1969

While Holland was a kingdom under Napoleon's brother Louis between 1806 and 1814 a number of Orders were created: the *Royal Order of the Union* (awarded to Dutchmen who had aided the French cause or French officials and officers serving in Holland), the *Royal Order of Merit* and the *Royal Order of Holland*. These had only a brief lifespan and became obsolete after the fall of Napoleon and the creation of the Kingdom of the Netherlands in 1815.

(Right) Netherlands: Order of Orange-Nassau. Neck Badge of a Commander, Civil Division.

(Above) Netherlands: Military Order of William. Knight's Breast Badge in silver, gold and enamel. The arms of the cross (obverse and reverse) bear the legend *Voor moed, belied, trouw* ('For courage, leadership, loyalty').

The nation's highest award for gallantry in battle is the *Military Order of William (Militaire Willemsorde)*, created by the new king, William I, in April 1815. It has four classes and can be conferred on civilians as well as military recipients for outstanding bravery in the face of the enemy. At its highest level it is the Dutch equivalent of the Victoria Cross.

Netherlands: Order of the Netherlands Lion. Sash Badge of the First Class. The motto is *Virtus nobilitat* ('Virtue ennobles').

The *Order of the Netherlands Lion* (*De Orde van Nederlandse Leeuw*), founded by William I in September 1815 in three classes, is essentially the highest-ranking award for civilians and is conferred for distinguished service to the state or achievement in the arts and sciences. It is conferred upon foreigners only for exceptional service.

The *Order of Orange-Nassau* (*De Orde van Oranje-Nassau*), named after the family titles and estates of Holland's ruling dynasty, was established in April 1892 by Emma, the Dowager Queen and Regent, in the name of her daughter, Queen Wilhelmina. The most commonly awarded Dutch Order, it has five classes and is conferred upon Dutch and foreign nationals who have rendered service to the Royal Family, the state or to society.

The *Royal Family Order of the House of Orange* (*De Huisorde van Oranje*), originally founded by Queen Wilhelmina in 1905 and re-established by Queen Juliana in 1969, is essentially a Royal Family Order conferred for meritorious service to the monarchy. It has three classes.

NORWAY

The powerful medieval kingdom of Norway was united with both Sweden and Denmark from 1389 to 1450, with Denmark from 1450 to 1814 and with Sweden from 1814 to 1905. In 1814, at the close of the Napoleonic Wars, Denmark was separated but Norway remained united with Sweden (very much as the junior partner) until 1905, when Norway broke away and emerged as a separate kingdom. Under German occupation from 1940 to 1945, Norway remains a constitutional monarchy.

> *The Order of St Olaf*, 1847, 1905, 1928
> *The Order of the Norwegian Lion*, 1904–05

The principal Norwegian award – and the Kingdom's only Order – is the highly regarded and attractive *Order of St Olaf* (*Sankt Olav's Orden*), founded by King Oscar I of Norway and Sweden in August 1847 and retained when Norway became independent in 1905 under Haakon VII. It is named after Norway's patron saint, Olaf the Holy, who as king between 1015 and 1030 established Christianity in the country and is buried in Trondheim Cathedral. There are five classes, and awards are made only for the most exceptional civil or military service to the state.

The *Order of the Norwegian Lion*, established by Oscar II of Norway and Sweden in 1904, was intended to be Norway's highest award but in the event was short-lived – it was almost immediately rendered obsolete by Norway's secession in 1905.

Norway: Order of St Olaf. Sash Badge of the Grand Cross (First Class), Civil Division. The cross has the crowned 'O' for Olaf between the arms.

POLAND

Poland has a complex history. An independent kingdom after 1025, it became one of the great European powers of the Middle Ages, its armies instrumental in defeating the westward expansion of the Turks. It later fell victim to the ambitions of its neighbours and a series of partitions between 1772 and 1795 divided its territories between Russia, Austria and Prussia. It remained in name only as part of the Russian Empire. In 1919 the Treaty of Versailles recreated an independent Poland as a republic. Under German occupation from 1939 to 1945, it became a communist 'People's Republic' in 1947 but with the break-up of the Soviet bloc it again became an independent republic in 1990.

(Left) Poland: Order of the White Eagle. An early Breast Star, c.1820.

(Right) Poland: Order of St Stanislaus. Breast Star, pre-1830 type, with the original central monogram 'SAR' (for its founder *Stanislaus Augustus Rex*), which was altered to 'SS' (*Sanctus Stanislaus*) when the Order became a general Russian award in 1830.

Some of its early Orders were retained for use in Poland as part of the Russian Empire and some were adopted for use throughout the Empire after the unsuccessful Polish Revolution of 1830. Some Polish Orders – especially Polonia Restituta and Military Virtue – were produced abroad (e.g. in London during the Second World War) and there are considerable variations in quality.

Occasionally, Polish awards (especially Polonia Restituta) are found in British groups for 1939–45 service.

The Order of the White Eagle, 1325, 1705–95, 1921
The Order of St Stanislaus, 1765–95, 1831–1917
The Order of the Immaculate Conception of the Virgin Mary, 1634
The Order of Polonia Restituta, 1921, 1944
The Order of Military Virtue, 1792, 1919, 1944
The Order of the Grünwald Cross, 1944

The *Order of the White Eagle*, Poland's most prestigious award, was founded as early as 1325 by King Vladislav I on the occasion of his son's marriage to Princess Anna of Lithuania. Revived in 1705 by King August II, it became a Russian Order after the annexation of Poland, retained especially for service within Poland but also more widely issued. Following the Russian Revolution in 1917, the Order lapsed in Russia but it was re-established by the new Polish Republic in February 1921. In one class, it was awarded for the most exceptional service to the kingdom or republic and could be conferred on foreign nationals. (See also page 79.)

Like the *White Eagle*, the *Order of St Stanislaus* (or *Stanislas*) was originally a Polish award but was later absorbed into the Russian system. It was founded in 1765 by King Stanislaus Augustus Poniatowski and was named in honour of St Stanislaus (1030–69), patron saint of Poland. Until 1845, awards of all classes conferred hereditary nobility on their recipient, but this was restricted in 1845 to holders of the First Class. (See also page 79.)

The prestigious *Order of Military Virtue* (*Order Virtuti Militari*) was founded by King Stanislaus II in 1792 and continued to be conferred upon Poles after the Russian annexation. Retained by the new republic in 1919 and by the communist state in 1944, it remains Poland's highest reward for gallantry and distinguished military service. There are five classes. A lower-tier *Medal for Merit on the Field of Glory* in gold, silver or bronze is associated with this Order.

The *Order of Polonia Restituta* ('Poland restored') (*Order Odrodzenia Polski*), established in February 1921 in five classes, rewards outstanding service to the state, especially in the arts and sciences, literature, social work, industry, commerce and agriculture. It may also be awarded for bravery, but not in a military context. The Order was retained by the communist state in 1944 and remains the most widely awarded Polish Order, rather like Britain's Order of the British Empire.

The *Order of the Grünwald Cross* (*Order Krzyza Grunwaldu*) was created in 1944 to reward bravery in battle or for training Poland's forces. It recalls the Battle of Grünwald in 1410 when the Poles and Lithuanians defeated the Teutonic Knights. In three classes, it may also be conferred on foreigners or as a 'unit award' to regiments and was granted as an honour to the cities of Warsaw and Lublin, whose citizens distinguished themselves during the Second World War.

PORTUGAL

The former Roman province of Lusitania, Portugal was under Moorish occupation from the eighth century and only gradually freed itself to become an independent kingdom after 1139. Under Spanish rule from 1580 to 1640, it then became a separate monarchy under the Bragança dynasty. Portugal

Poland: Order of Military Virtue. Breast Badge. The reverse is often (but not always) individually numbered. This Order was regarded as Poland's highest military reward. During the Second World War, many of its five classes were conferred by the Polish Government in Exile (in Britain) on Polish personnel fighting alongside British and Allied forces.

became one of the great maritime trading powers of the Middle Ages and the centre of an empire in Brazil, Africa and the Far East. After a revolution in 1911 Portugal became a republic.

Its Orders constitute some of the most ancient and prestigious in Europe. Some were conferred on British officers for service in the Peninsular War (1808–14) and some are occasionally seen in British groups for 1914–18. Many underwent alterations to their design when Portugal became a republic in 1911.

Portugal: Military Order of Christ. Commander's Neck Badge and Breast Star. The distinctive cross used as the Badge of the Order is a Latin cross with triangular ends. It hangs from an elaborate 'bleeding heart' suspension. The Breast Star of this Order (left) is also very distinctive in design.

The Military Order of Christ, 1318, 1522, 1789, 1918

The Military Order of St Benedict (or *St Bento*) *of Aviz*, 1144, 1162, 1789, 1910

The Military Order of St James of the Sword (or *of Compostella*), 1290, 1320, 1789, 1910

The Military Order of the Tower and the Sword, 1459, 1808, 1832, 1917

The Order of the Empire, 1932

The Order of Our Lady of Villa Vicosa, 1819–1911

The Order of St Isabella, 1801–1911

The Order of Merit, 1929

The Order for Public Instruction, 1919

The Order of Industrial and Agricultural Merit, 1893, 1926

(Left) Portugal. Unusually, recipients of both the Order of St Benedict of Aviz and the Order of Christ can wear a single 'combined' Badge. Shown here is a Sash Badge that represents no fewer than three Portuguese Orders – as worn by recipients of the Orders of Christ, St Benedict of Aviz and St James of the Sword. Unsurprisingly, insignia representing these double or triple awards are rare.

(Right) Portugal: Order of the Tower and the Sword. Grand Cross Collar Chain in silver-gilt and enamel, by da Souza of Lisbon.

Portugal's oldest and most prestigious award is the *Military Order of Christ* (*Ordem Militar do Cristo*). Founded as early as 1318 by King Denis (or Dionysius), it is unusual in that like the Burgundian Golden Fleece (q.v.) it was also awarded by another state; in this case, the Order was confirmed in 1319 by Pope John XXII and thereafter also conferred by the Papacy. In 1522 a separate Portuguese version was established. Originally a military award, it briefly became obsolete when the Republic was founded in 1911, but it was re-established with a different design in 1918 and continues to be awarded for exceptional service. It has three classes and can be conferred on foreigners.

The *Order of St Benedict of Aviz* (*Ordem Militar d'Aviz*), another ancient foundation originally established *c*.1144 as the Order of Evora, rewarded civil and military merit. It has three classes. An unusual award was the combined *Order of Christ and St Benedict of Aviz*, founded in one class by King Denis and worn by those who held *both* the Order of Christ and the Order of Aviz; its insignia combine the emblems of both Orders.

Even older than these, though ranked slightly lower, is the *Military Order of St James of the Sword* (*Ordem Militar de Sant'Iago da Espada*). Derived from a Spanish Order, it was established as a separate Portuguese award by King Denis in 1290 and is one of the oldest still conferred. Originally awarded

(Left) Portugal: Order of Our Lady of Villa Vicosa. Sash Badge in silver-gilt and enamel. The central medallion has the letters 'MA' for Maria and the legend *Padroeira do Reino* ('Patroness of the kingdom').

(Right) Portugal: Order of St Isabella. The attractive Breast Badge of this single-class Order, *c*.1850. The central medallion has a delicate scene in enamels showing the saint giving alms to a beggar. It is surrounded by a wreath of laurel and roses above the legend *Pauperum solatio* ('I comfort the poor').

for special service to the Catholic Church, it was secularised in 1789 and since 1862 has been conferred in five classes on citizens or foreigners for achievement in the arts, science and literature.

The *Military Order of the Tower and the Sword* (*Ordem Militar da Tôrre e Espada*) was established in 1459 by Alfonso V as the Order of the Sword after his conquest of Fez in Morocco. It lapsed for generations but was revived in 1808 as the Military Order of the Tower and the Sword. Intended for service in the Portuguese colony of Brazil, it became a general award for civil or military merit and was awarded, for example, to British officers in Portuguese service during the Peninsular War, 1808–14. It had five classes.

The *Order of Our Lady of Villa Vicosa* (*Ordem Villa Vicosa*) was established in 1819 as a military or civil reward, principally for service in Brazil and to Portuguese-Americans. Named after the Virgin Mary, patroness of Portugal, it became obsolete in 1911 when the republic was founded. Another Order that became obsolete in 1911 was the *Order of St Isabella*, established in 1801 by Prince John VI on the suggestion of his wife, Princess Charlotte, as a reward for Roman Catholic ladies who had undertaken significant charitable work. It had only one class and was restricted to twenty-six members, who had to be of noble birth.

A series of Orders was created to reward merit in various professions and walks of life. The *Order of Industrial and Agricultural Merit* (*Ordem do Mérito Agricola e Industrial*) (1893) is unusual in having two divisions, one for agriculture and one for industry, each with different insignia but within one Order. Each division has four classes and a lower-tier Medal. The *Order of Public Instruction* (*Ordem da Instrucao Publica*) (1919) rewards teachers and civil servants and has four classes and an associated Medal. The *Order of Merit* (*Ordem da Benemerencia*) (1929) is awarded for outstanding service in the fields of administration, public health, industry and welfare. There are four classes and an associated lower-tier Medal.

The *Order of the Empire* (*Ordem do Imperio*), established in five classes as late as 1932, was intended to reward service in or to Portugal's extensive overseas empire. Often awarded to colonial civil servants and diplomats, it can also be conferred on foreigners.

PRUSSIA

The growth of Prussia, derived from the territory of the ancient Borussi, from whom it was named, was linked with the rise of the Teutonic Knights in eastern Europe and it grew slowly during the Middle Ages. As the state of Brandenburg, under the Hohenzollerns from 1415 to 1918, it became a duchy in 1618 and a kingdom from 1710 to 1918. Prussia gradually expanded by alliance and conquest to weld together the many German states to found the German Empire, proclaimed in 1871 after the defeat of France in the Franco-Prussian War. From 1871 to 1918 the Kings of Prussia were also Emperors of Germany. With the defeat of Germany, Prussia became a Free State in 1918 but was abolished as a state in 1947.

Brandenburg (Princely State or Palatinate to 1710)
The Order of Sincerity (*L'Ordre de la Sincerité*), 1705
The Order of Concord (*L'Ordre de la Concorde*), 1660
The Order of Generosity (*L'Ordre de la Générosité*), 1667

Prussia (Kingdom from 1710 to 1918)
The Order of the Black Eagle, 1701
The Order of the Red Eagle, 1734
The Military Order Pour le Mérite, 1740, 1810
The Order Pour le Mérite for Arts and Science, 1842
The Order of the Crown of Prussia, 1861
The Royal House Order of Hohenzollern, 1841, 1851
The Order of Louise, 1813, 1848, 1865
The Order of the Swan, 1843
The Order of Merit of the Crown of Prussia, 1901
The Iron Cross, 1813, 1870, 1914, 1939-45
The Order of Wilhelm, 1896
The Saxe-Ernestine Order, 1690, 1833

Prussia's highest Decoration was the *Order of the Black Eagle* (*Orden vom Schwarzen Adler*), founded by her first king, Frederick I, in January 1701 to reward outstanding service, military or civil. Originally it was conferred only on the aristocracy but from 1847 a recipient automatically received hereditary nobility.

Perhaps the most famous Prussian Order is the military *Pour le Mérite*, later nicknamed the 'Blue Max'. Founded in May 1667 by the Elector Frederick (later Frederick I, the first King of Prussia) as a reward at the highest level, it originated as the Brandenburg *Order of Generosity*. It was revived under its new name by Frederick II in 1740 and altered by Frederick III in 1810 to a purely military award, granted for outstanding bravery in battle. From 1870 to 1918, as a Prussian award available to all German forces, it was effectively the equivalent of the Victoria Cross. It was not conferred after 1918. A civil version was created in Prussia in 1842 to reward outstanding national achievement in the arts or science. This too lapsed in 1918 but was revived in West Germany in 1951 and continues to be awarded. Restricted to one class and only thirty holders at any one time, it may be conferred on foreigners as honorary members.

The *Order of the Red Eagle* (*Der Rote Adlerorden*) originated in November 1705 as the *Order of Sincerity*, founded by Prince George William of Bayreuth-Brandenburg. Refounded in 1734 as the Order of the Red Eagle, it was adopted as a fully Prussian award in June 1792, extended to three classes in 1810 and to four in 1830. The Order could be conferred on foreigners and there were some British recipients, sometimes honoured for service to the Prussian/German Royal Family.

(Left) Prussia: Order of Louise. Breast Badge of c.1865 worn from a ladies' bow. Founded in 1813 as a reward to women for meritorious and charitable work, this Order was infrequently conferred and examples from before 1914–18 (when rather more were awarded for war work) are rare.

(Right) Prussia: Order of the Black Eagle. The Sash Badge of this single-class Order is a handsome piece in blue enamel; the arms of the cross are linked by the black eagles of the Order's title.

(Left) Prussia: Military Order *Pour le Mérite*. Neck Badge. Commonly known as the 'Blue Max', this well-known single-class Order was the highest award for military gallantry and was bestowed, for example, on Germany's greatest war heroes and air aces during the First World War.

(Right) Prussia: Order of the Red Eagle. Neck Badge of the Second Class, Military Division, in silver-gilt and enamel.

The *Order of the Crown of Prussia* (*Kronenorden*) was founded on the day of his coronation (18th October 1861) by William I of Prussia. In five classes, it rewarded outstanding civil or military service. The one-class *Order of Wilhelm* (*Wilhelmsorden*), conferred mainly on foreign heads of state, or on Germans for especially meritorious service, was established by the Emperor William II in 1896. The Badge, a gold medallion bearing the profile of William I, was worn from a gold collar bearing the wording *WILHELMUS I REX* in white enamel and had no ribbon or Breast Star.

The *Royal House Order of Hohenzollern* (*Fürstlicher Hausorden von Hohenzollern*) originated in 1841 as the Princely House Order of Hohenzollern, an award created in the small state of Hohenzollern (from which the Prussian ruling dynasty originated). It was extended to form the Royal House Order when the state was absorbed into Prussia and was essentially awarded for service to the Royal Family. (See illustration on page 9.)

The *Order of Merit of the Crown of Prussia* (*Verdienst Orden der Preussichen Krone*) was established by William II in January 1901 as an award in one class for civil or military merit. It was rarely awarded.

For the *Iron Cross* (*Eisernes Kreuz*) see Nazi Germany.

ROMANIA

The Balkan province of Romania (or Rumania, or Roumania), bordering the Black Sea, was part of the Turkish Empire from the mid fifteenth century. After the Crimean War (1854–56) it was united with the provinces of Moldavia and Wallachia, granted the status of principality in 1866 and became a monarchy in 1881. Its monarchy (along with its Royal Orders) was abolished in 1948 and Romania became a communist 'People's Republic' within the Soviet sphere. With the collapse of Soviet power, Romania re-emerged as a republic in 1989.

Romania created an extensive range of distinctive Orders, which, like those of Bulgaria, reflect the styles of other European awards, especially German and French; many earlier types were made by Austrian jewellers. Romanian Orders were occasionally awarded to British recipients for service in 1914–18, but these are rare. During the Second World War, as a German ally, many of its awards were conferred on officers and officials of the Axis powers. As with other states in the communist bloc, Romania produced a large number of Orders after 1948.

The Order of Carol I, 1906–47

The Order of St Michael the Brave, 1916–47

The Order of the Star of Romania, 1877, 1932–47

The Order of the Crown of Romania, 1881, 1932–47

The Order of Ferdinand I, 1929–47

The Order for Faithful Service, 1932–47

The Order of Merit for Science and the Arts, 1931

The Order of Agricultural Merit, 1932

The Romanian Order of Hohenzollern (or *Royal Household Order*), 1931–47

The Royal Household Order Bene Merenti, 1932/35–47

The Order of Merit, 1932

The Military Order of Michael the Brave, 1916

The Order of Aeronautical Merit, 1930–47

(Left) Romania: Order of the Star of Romania. The attractive Badge (that of the Grand Cross is shown) carries in the centre the Order's motto, *In fide salus* ('Salvation lies in fidelity'). The reverse centre has the cipher of its founder, Carol (Charles) I.

(Right) Romania: Cross of the Order of Elizabeth, 1878. The Order was awarded only to ladies, for charitable work.

Romania: Order of the Crown. The Sash Badge and Breast Star of the First Class (Grand Cross).

The Military Order of St George, 1940–47
The Order for Culture and Freedom, 1933
The Order of the Provincial Guard, 1935
The Order of Elizabeth, 1878

The *Order of the Star of Romania* (*Ordinul Steaua Romaniei*) was the first Romanian Order to be founded after her self-proclaimed independence and was based on an earlier Unification Order established in the provinces of Moldavia and Wallachia *c.*1860. When Carol I acceded to the throne in 1881 he confirmed the award in five classes. As is common, military awards bore crossed swords through the design and, rather unusually within the European system of orders, posthumous awards were possible. During the Second World War, it could also be conferred as a 'unit citation', e.g. on whole regiments. The Badge was redesigned in 1932 and its ribbon altered in 1938.

The *Order of Elizabeth*, founded as early as 1878 as the Commemorative and Meritorious Cross, was awarded only to ladies for meritorious and charitable work.

Romania's highest award was the *Order of Carol I*, established by that king in March 1906 for distinguished service. In four classes, its First Class (Grand Cross) was reserved for the Royal Family and foreign heads of state. An earlier foundation of Carol I (March 1881) was the *Order of the Crown of Romania* (*Ordinul Coroana Romaniei*), awarded in five classes, originally to civil servants and officials for outstanding service to the kingdom. The Badges exist in two distinct design versions – 1881–1932 and 1932–47 – and a military division was added in 1938.

The Order of St Michael the Brave, born out of the conditions of the First World War, was established in December 1916 by Ferdinand I as a reward for meritorious service in war (see illustration on page 6). Most of its later recipients were German officers in the Second World War, when Romania was an ally of the Third Reich.

King Carol II (ruled 1930–40) established a number of new awards. He instituted the distinctive *Order of Ferdinand I* in 1929 in honour of his father. In five classes, it rewarded civil merit whilst the *Order for Faithful Service* (*Servicil Credincios*) rewarded loyal service to the Crown and Royal Family. Founded in 1932, it had four classes. The *Order of Merit for Science and the Arts* (1931) and the *Order of Agricultural Merit* (1932), each in five classes, rewarded achievement in their respective spheres and professions whilst the *Order of Aeronautical Merit* (1930) rewarded not only outstanding aviators, military and civil, but also those who contributed to the development of Romania's military and civilian aviation.

THE RUSSIAN EMPIRE

The medieval states of Russia were overrun by the Mongols after 1242 and remained under their rule until one state, Muscovy (Moscow), established its supremacy. From 1328, it expanded to create an increasingly large kingdom. The country was under Romanov rule from 1613 to 1917 and gradually established a powerful empire. The Russian Revolution of 1917 led to the creation of the first communist state, which in 1922 became the Union of Soviet Socialist Republics (USSR) and after 1945 the centre of a European communist bloc. Since the collapse of the USSR in 1991, its associated states have broken away, leaving Russia as an independent federal republic with a nascent democracy.

The Russian Empire produced a large range of Orders, many of which were also awarded in its imperial territories such as Poland and Finland. They constitute one of the most attractive and collected series of Orders, their workmanship generally being of the highest quality, manufactured by leading jewellers in Russia and Paris. Many were awarded to British recipients, especially for 1914–18 service, when Russia was one of the Allied Powers.

Some Tsarist awards continued to be conferred by 'White Russian' (monarchist) commanders during the Russian Civil War (1918–21) and were given to British officers and other ranks involved in the Allied intervention at that time. These insignia are, hardly surprisingly, often of inferior quality. Only one new Tsarist award was created after the Civil War by royalist forces in exile; this was the *Order of St Nicholas, Creator of Peace* (1929), a reward for continued service to the monarchist cause. Examples are rare.

All Tsarist Orders became obsolete on the establishment of the

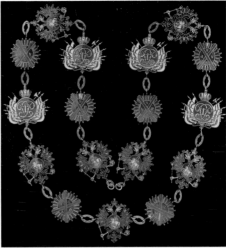

communist state, but most of their ribbon types were revived for new awards and it is interesting that the egalitarian communist regime itself established a large range of Orders, rewarding service in every walk of life. Some of these were awarded to British recipients for service in 1939–45.

See also the Union of Soviet Socialist Republics, below.

(Left) Russia: Order of St Andrew the First-Named. The attractive Sash Badge of this single-class Order, by Keibel of St Petersburg, c.1865.

(Right) Russia: Order of St Andrew the First Named. The magnificent Collar or Chain of the Grand Cross, by Keibel of St Petersburg, late nineteenth century.

The Order of St Andrew the First-Named, 1698
The Order of St Catherine, 1714
The Order of St Alexander Nevsky, 1725
The Order of St Anne, 1735, 1797
The Military Order of the Great Martyr and Victor, St George, 1769
The Order of St Vladimir, 1782
The Order of the White Eagle, 1705 (Poland), 1815 (Russian Poland), 1830
The Order of St Stanislas, 1765 (Poland), 1815 (Russian Poland), 1830
The Red Cross Order, 1878
The Order of Agricultural Merit, 1878

Some of Russian's Tsarist Orders were among the most exclusive ever instituted, conferred only on the highest ranks of the aristocracy, senior officials of the government or Orthodox Church, senior diplomats, foreign dignitaries or military officers. Some of them were associated with a range of other awards – unlike anything else in Europe – such as Swords of Honour, sword knots, daggers, silverware, medallions worn at the sword hilt, grants of land, elevation through the ranks of the nobility, etc. Such awards were often decorated with the ribbon or colours of the Order. Similarly decorated 'unit awards' – such as presentation trumpets or swords – were also made to distinguished regiments.

The first and most prestigious Russian award was the *Order of St Andrew the First-Named*, founded by Peter the Great in November 1698 as part of his westernisation of the country. It was named after the patron saint of Russia and always bestowed personally by the Tsar. Its one class (with a Collar, Badge and Star) was reserved for monarchs or the highest ranks of the nobility, and recipients automatically became Knights of the Orders of St Alexander Nevsky and the White Eagle and received the First Class of the Orders of St Anne and St Stanislas. On insignia for non-Christians the image of the crucified St Andrew was replaced by the Imperial Russian eagle.

The *Order of St Alexander Nevsky* was named after the military leader and saint (1220–63) who led the Russians against the Swedes and Teutonic Knights and it depicts the hero on horseback. In one class, and primarily a military distinction, it was originally proposed by Peter the Great but was not established until 1725 by his wife and successor, Catherine I.

The *Order of St Anne* was founded in Kiel in 1735 by the Duke of Schleswig-Holstein in honour of his wife Anna, daughter of Peter the Great, and was often bestowed on Russians. In 1797 it was adopted as a purely Russian award, largely for long and meritorious service, and, though originally a civil decoration, was extended for war service in 1855 during the Crimean War. It was awarded in three classes, but there was effectively a Fourth Class in the form of an enamelled medallion inscribed 'For bravery' and worn on the sword hilt. Up to 1845, all holders received hereditary

(Left) Russia: Order of St Alexander Nevsky. The Sash Badge, by Keibel of St Petersburg, c.1900, of this single-class Order is typical of the fine-quality design and workmanship that characterise Tsarist Russian Orders.

(Right) Russia: Order of St Anne. Two types of Badge: a civil award (left), and the military version 'with swords' (right). (See also illustrations on page 13.)

nobility, but after this only recipients of the First Class received this honour since it was felt that too many were being conferred. Recipients of the lower classes of the Order received only 'life' nobility.

Both the *Order of the White Eagle* and the *Order of St Stanislas* (or *Stanislaus*) were originally Polish awards (q.v.), established in 1705 and 1765, but after the unsuccessful Polish revolution of 1830 Poland was formally absorbed into Russia and both Orders became general Russian awards. The latter, with its dark red enamel and gold Badge, is exceptionally beautiful in design; in three classes, it has variant designs for Christian and non-Christian recipients and had Medals of different classes associated as lower-tier awards for non-officer recipients. As with the Order of St Anne, the St Stanislas carried the right to hereditary nobility until 1845, after which only holders of the First Class received this honour.

The *Military Order of the Great Martyr and Victor, St George* was founded by Empress Catherine the Great in 1769, essentially as an award for bravery in battle or outstanding military merit, and was not conferred on civilians except for service under enemy fire. It conferred an array of awards, depending on the rank or achievement of the recipient. For example, magnificent Swords of Honour, bearing the ribbon of the Order, could be conferred on high-ranking officers for services of national importance. The Order itself had four classes, but associated with it were 'Insignia of Military Distinction' commonly known as the Cross of St George. These were

(Left) Russia: Order of the White Eagle. The elaborate Sash Badge of the First Class, by Keibel of St Petersburg, in gold and enamel, c.1900.

(Right) Russia: Order of St Stanislas. This example of the beautiful Neck Badge of the Order is in black enamel; red was more common. In the post-1830 Russian version, the centre has 'SS' for St Stanislas, replacing the 'SAR' (*Stanislas Augustus Rex*) of the original Polish version.

(Top left) Russia: Order of St George the Martyr. The Insignia of Military Distinction, commonly known as the Cross of St George, Third Class, with bow, c.1914–16. The Crosses and associated Medals are usually numbered, reflecting the fact that originally a register of the recipients was kept.

(Top right) Russia: Order of St George. Sash Badge of the Grand Cross (First Class), c.1850.

(Bottom left) Russia: Order of St Vladimir. Fourth Class Breast Badge of the Military Division (i.e. 'with swords'), made in St Petersburg, c.1914–17. The ribbon is worn in typical Russian fashion.

awarded to lower ranks for bravery in action, in one class after 1807 and four classes after 1856 (gold, with or without ribbon bow, or silver, with or without bow). There were also four lower-tier Medals of St George in gold or silver, with or without bows, instituted in 1878. Both carried additional

(Bottom Right) Russia: Order of St Catherine. A beautiful jewelled example of the Neck Badge, by Keibel of St Petersburg, c.1870. The oval medallion of the saint, finely depicted in enamels, is surrounded by a band of seventeen diamonds, with twenty-nine others set around the badge.

pay and pensions. Some two million Crosses or Medals were conferred for 1914–17 service and many were awarded to British recipients for service around Ypres in 1914–15 or at the naval Battle of Jutland in May 1916. Its ribbon was reused for the Soviet Order of Glory (q.v.).

The distinctive *Order of St Vladimir*, founded by Catherine the Great in 1782 in four classes, commemorated the saint who introduced Christianity to Russia. It was conferred for a wide variety of services, e.g. saving the lives of 'more than ten people', loyal service to the state for thirty-five years or major achievement in the arts or professions. Originally intended as a civil award, it was, like the Order of St George, extended to reward military service in 1855 during the Crimean War, in which case crossed swords pierced the Badge.

The *Order of St Catherine* was created by Peter the Great in 1714 to perpetuate the memory of the remarkable actions of his mistress, Catherine, in freeing the Tsar and an entire Russian army from the Turks in 1712. She eventually became Tsarina and ruled briefly (1725–27) as Catherine I after Peter's death. The Order was instituted on her name day, 24th November, and named in honour of St Catherine of Alexandria. Its two classes were awarded only to ladies of the highest rank, Russian or foreign, and rarely conferred.

SAN MARINO

A city state in central Italy, this small republic was founded in the ninth century and recognised as independent from 1631. Since the unification of Italy, 1860–70, San Marino has been under Italian protection but remains an independent state.

> *The Equestrian (Knights') Order of St Marinus* (or *San Marino*), 1859
> *The Order of Knights of St Agatha*, 1923

The principal Order is the *Equestrian Order of St Marinus* (*Ordine Equestri di San Marino*), founded in August 1859. It rewards distinguished civil or military service or achievement in the arts and sciences and is conferred mainly on foreigners. It is named after the traditional founder of the state, St Marino or Marinus, a simple stonemason who established the first religious community on Mount Titano (now named after him as San Marino). It has five classes; its Grand Cross is conferred only upon heads of state.

The *Order of Knights of St Agatha* (*Ordine Equestri di Sant'Agatha*) was established in June 1923 to reward civil or military service and again is conferred mainly on foreigners. It too has five classes and is named after St Agatha, depicted on the Badges of the Order, who with St Marino is patron saint of the state. In 1740, on the 5th February (the feast day of St Agatha), Pope Clement XII reconfirmed the independence of the Republic.

San Marino: Equestrian Order of St Marinus. Knight's Breast Badge of the Civil Division (without swords), in silver-gilt and enamel. Around the central profile of the country's patron saint is the legend *San Marino protector.*

SERBIA

The powerful Balkan kingdom of Serbia came under Turkish rule after 1459, achieving a measure of independence only in 1829. It was under Austrian occupation during the First World War but by the Treaty of St Germain in 1919 was established as the dominant partner in the new Kingdom of Yugoslavia, which amalgamated several Balkan states. Under German occupation from 1941 to 1945, Yugoslavia became a communist republic in 1945 but with the Balkan Wars of the 1990s the country was fragmented and Serbia emerged as an independent republic.

Most of Serbia's Orders were manufactured in Vienna before 1918 and afterwards in Switzerland.

As an Allied power, Serbia's Orders (especially the White Eagle and St Sava) are sometimes seen in British groups for service in the First World War.

Unusually, it was decreed in the First World War that all Serbian awards for military service should be worn from a plain red ribbon – which means that a recipient of a number of Serbian orders for 1914–18 would wear simply a row of red ribbons with no distinguishing marks.

See also Yugoslavia, below.

The Order of St Lazarus, 1882
The Royal Order of Milos the Great, 1899–1903
The Order of Takovo, 1865–1903
The Order of the White Eagle, 1882
The Order of St Sava, 1883–1945

(Left) Serbia: Royal Order of Milos the Great. The Breast Star of this rare Order. The central medallion of this example (by Fischmeister of Vienna) is beautifully executed, with a portrait of the Serbian hero, suspended from the crown of the Nemanya dynasty, the late medieval rulers of Serbia under Turkish suzerainty.

(Right) Serbia: Order of St Sava. First Class Sash Badge. The arms of Serbia appear between the limbs of the cross.

The Red Cross Order, 1878
The Order of the Karageorge Star (or *Karageorgeovich*), 1903

(Left) Serbia: Order of Takovo. An attractive Fourth Class Breast Badge with central cipher of Milan Obrenovitch III, in silver-gilt and enamel.

(Right) Serbia: Order of the White Eagle. The beautiful Sash Badge and Breast Star of the Grand Cross (First Class), Military Division, with crossed swords, c.1915. Awarded in all classes and in some numbers to British officers during the First World War, it is perhaps the most familiar of Serbian orders.

Founded by Serbia's first king, Milan I (ruled 1868–89), the *Order of St Lazarus* is possibly the most exclusive of all Orders since it could be worn only by the King himself. Unsurprisingly, examples are exceptionally rare.

The *Royal Order of Milos the Great*, founded by Alexander I (ruled 1889–1903), was Serbia's highest Decoration after St Lazarus, rewarding services to the Royal Family, the Obrenovich dynasty. It lapsed following the King's assassination in 1903 and the accession of the Karageorge dynasty, effectively being replaced by the Order of the Karageorge Star (below). There were four classes. The Badge was an oval gold medallion with a hand-painted image of the Serbian hero of 1815, Milos the Great.

Given the exclusivity of the Order of St Lazarus and the short life of the Order of Milos the Great, the *Order of the White Eagle* was effectively Serbia's highest-ranking honour. Established by Milan I in 1882, it was awarded for outstanding civil or military service and had five classes. Its attractive Badge takes the form of a white enamelled double-headed eagle bearing at its centre the arms of Serbia. When awarded for war service, it bore crossed swords below its crown suspension. Considerable numbers – especially of the fourth and fifth classes – were awarded to British officers during the First World War, so it is quite often seen among British medal groups.

Serbia: Order of the Karageorge Star. Grand Officer's Neck Badge and Breast Star of the Military Division, 'with swords'. The central legend, around the arms of Serbia, is 'For honour and liberty' in Cyrillic script.

The *Order of Takovo* was the oldest of Serbia's Decorations, founded by Prince Michael in 1865 when Serbia was beginning to cast off Turkish rule, and was primarily an award for military merit. As usual with Serbian orders, there were five classes. The Badge, an eight-pointed cross of white enamel pierced by a St Andrew's cross, bore in a central medallion the founder's cipher and the inscription 'For faith, prince and fatherland'.

The *Order of St Sava* was founded in February 1883 by Milan I and takes its name from the patron saint of Serbia (1174–1237), the founder of the national church and one of its principal cultural heroes. Awarded in the usual five classes, it was granted for outstanding achievement in art, science, literature, religion or social work. With the establishment of a communist regime in Yugoslavia in 1945, all former Serbian orders were abolished, but this award continued to be conferred by the last King, Peter II, in exile, until his death in 1970. The Badge's central medallion shows St Sava surrounded by a blue band on which is inscribed in Cyrillic script 'By his talents he acquired all'. There are variants in the design, with the saint shown in either red or yellow robes.

The *Order of the Karageorge Star*, established by Peter I in 1904 on the accession the Karageorgeovich dynasty, was intended to replace the Royal Order of Milos the Great (above) as an award for the most distinguished military or civil service. There were four classes. When it was awarded for war service, crossed swords pierced the Badge in saltire fashion. As with other Serbian awards, during the First World War its usual ribbon (red edged with white) was replaced by a plain red version.

SLOVAKIA

Slovakia became part of Czechoslovakia in 1919 but during the Second World War was a Nazi puppet state. After the war, it resumed its status as part of Czechoslovakia but with the fragmentation of the Soviet bloc it broke away to form the Republic of Slovakia in 1992. Its only Orders (apart from any instituted since then) were the creations of Monsignor Josef Tiso, its pro-Nazi leader, and ceased to be awarded after 1944.

The Order of Prince Pribina, 1940–44
The Order of the Slovak Cross, 1940–44
The Order of the Victorious War Cross, 1940–44

The *Order of Prince Pribina* (*Rad Knietzata Pribinu*), established in March 1939, was named after the first ruler of an independent Slovak state and the founder of its Catholic Church in the ninth century. It was awarded mainly to German and Italian military and civilian dignitaries for war service and such awards bear crossed swords. The *Order of the Slovak Cross* (May 1940) depicts Father Andrew Hlinka, a leading Slovak writer and nationalist, notorious for his terrorisation of opponents through the Hlinka Guards. In six classes, it was awarded for civil and military services, but few seem to have been conferred.

Little is known about the *Order of the Victorious War Cross*.

SOVEREIGN ORDERS

During the early Middle Ages, several powerful Orders of Knighthood were given temporal powers of administration and government as 'Sovereign Orders'. The main ones were the *Order of St Lazarus*, the *Orthodox Order of the Holy Sepulchre* (based in Jerusalem), the famous *Knights Templars* and the very powerful *Teutonic Knights*. All had their own insignia but all were more or less suppressed or lost their power by the late Middle Ages. The only one that survives in any significant way – and retains a system of awards – is the *Order of St John of Jerusalem* (see Malta).

SPAIN

The Roman province of Hispania and later a Visigothic kingdom, Spain came under Moorish occupation from 711. The northern Christian kingdoms (like Castile) gradually freed the country from Moorish rule during the medieval *Reconquista* and the last Moorish province, Grenada, was conquered in 1492, when Spain became a unified kingdom. One of the great military and imperial powers of Europe, it was under Hapsburg rule from 1516 to 1700 and largely under Bourbon rule from 1700 to 1931. A republic from 1931 (under General Franco, 1936–75), Spain became a monarchy again in 1976.

(Left) Spain: Military Order of St James of the Sword. Breast Badge – a beautiful, privately commissioned piece of c.1875, the stylised sword set with seventy-seven red gemstones.

(Right) Spain: Royal and Military Order of St Hermengildo. Breast Star of the Grand Cross, in silver gilt, gold and enamel, c.1850.

Over the centuries Spain has produced a bewildering number of Orders, probably more than any other European state. Also, during the Middle Ages there were many 'Corporations of Knighthood' – effectively societies founded by minor noblemen or magnates, which conferred their own awards. Examples are the *Order of the Lily of Navarre* (1034?), the *Order of the Fish Scales* (1318), the *Order of the Lily of Aragon* (1410), and many more that are outside the scope of the present work. The majority were short-lived.

Some of Spain's Orders are very ancient. Many were abolished when Spain became a republic in 1931 but were re-established under General Franco after 1936 and remain in use. He also instituted a wide range of new Orders, initially as rewards for service to his cause.

The Order of the Golden Fleece, 1430 (Burgundy), 1721 (separate Spanish branch), 1931; re-established 1976

The Imperial Order of the Yoke and Arrows, 1937, 1943

The Order of Charles III, 1771, 1814, 1942

The Royal and Military Order of St Hermengildo, 1814

The Royal and Military Order of St Ferdinand, 1815, 1920, 1940

The Order of Isabella the Catholic, 1815, 1938

The Order of the Cross of St Raimund de Peñaforte, 1944

The Royal and Military Order of Maria Christina, 1890

The Civil Order of Alfonso X, the Wise, 1939

The Order of Military Merit, 1864

The Order of Naval Merit, 1866

The Order of Civil Merit, 1926, 1942

The Civil Order of Public Health, 1922, 1943

The Order of Agricultural Merit, 1905, 1939

The Civil Order of Charity, 1856

The Military Order of St James of the Sword, 1170

The Military Order of Calatrava, 1158, 1808, 1874

The Military Order of Alcantara, 1156, 1523, 1808

The Military Order of Our Lady of Montesa, 1319

The Sovereign Order of St John of Jerusalem, 1118

The Civil Order of Alfonso XII, 1902–31

The Order of Cisneros, 1944

The Order of Africa, 1933

The Order of Isabella the Second, 1833

The Civil Order of Maria Victoria, 1871 (for arts and science)

The Royal Order of Queen Maria Louisa, 1792

The Order of Love, 1870

The Royal Spanish Order of Joseph Bonaparte, 1808

The Order of Merit of the Spanish Republic, 1933

(Left) Spain: Imperial Order of the Yoke and Arrows. Part of the Collar. The motto of the Order is *Caesaris Caesari Dei Deo* ('Render unto Caesar that which is Caesar's and to God that which is God's).

(Right) Spain: Royal and Military Order of St Ferdinand. The Breast Badge of an Officer (i.e. Fourth Class) (left) and the Breast Star (right), in silver, with gold and enamel centre, set with jewels.

The three most ancient Spanish Orders are still conferred: the *Military Order of St James of the Sword* (1170) – which also has a Portuguese version; the *Military Order of Alcantara* (c.1156); and the *Military Order of Calatrava* (1158). They originated as Military Orders whose members were dedicated to service against the Moors, then occupying most of Spain, and the last two are still conferred as awards for military merit.

As in Austria, the Burgundian *Order of the Golden Fleece (Orden del Toison de*

(Left) Spain: Order of Isabella the Catholic. The beautifully worked Breast Star of the Grand Cross, in silver, gold and enamels. There is a great deal of variation between manufacturers in the quality of enamel work in all European insignia, but this example is of the highest quality.

(Right) Spain: Order of Naval Merit. Breast Star, by Castells of Barcelona, in silver, silver-gilt and enamel. The Badge of the Order is essentially the central device carried on the star. Awards for military or war service have red enamel, and those for peacetime or non-combatant service have white enamel.

Oro) (1430) was and is Spain's premier Order, re-established as recently as 1976. The Order descended in the Hapsburg monarchies of both Spain and Austria and was conferred by both houses, a situation given official sanction in 1721 after generations of dispute as to the status of the award. The Duke of Wellington was one recipient, for his service in the liberation of Spain during the Peninsular War. (See illustration on page 23.)

The *Imperial Order of the Yoke and Arrows* (*Orden Imperial del Yugo y las Flechas*), a new Order established under the dictator General Franco in October 1937, was initially a high-ranking award for service to Franco and his Falangist party during the Spanish Civil War; it later became a general reward for political services. There were four classes. It outranked the 'Royal and Illustrious' *Order of Charles III* (*Orden de Carlos III*), founded by that king in September 1771 in commemoration of the birth of his grandson. This was a much altered and amended Order, frequently re-instituted. It was finally refounded by Franco in 1942; its five classes reward outstanding service to the state by Spaniards or foreigners. In an unusual reversal of the normal precedence, its Fifth Class ranks as the highest grade, the First Class as the lowest.

Ferdinand VII revived or established a number of orders in 1814–15 following the Napoleonic occupation of Spain between 1808 and 1814. The *Royal and Military Order of St Hermengildo* (*Real y Militar Orden de San Hermengildo*) rewarded officers for long and meritorious service in Spain's armed forces. In three classes, it was named after the Visigothic leader and Christian martyr St Hermengildo or Hermengilde. The Duke of Wellington also received this Order – among many others. The *Royal and Military Order of St Ferdinand* (*Real y Militar Orden de San Fernando*) commemorated the King's ancestor Ferdinand II (1220–52). It is open to all ranks of the Spanish army for meritorious service and has five classes. One version of its Breast Star is unusual in comprising simply four swords, hilt to hilt, forming a cross. The *Order of Isabella the Catholic* (*Orden de Isabel la Catolica*) was primarily a reward for service in Spain's South American colonies but later became a reward for civil or military merit in any area. Its name recalls Queen and Saint Isabella of Castile, who with Ferdinand of Aragon ruled, as the 'Catholic Kings', the newly united Spain after the final expulsion of the Moors in 1492.

The *Royal and Military Order of Maria Christina* (*Real y Militar Orden de Maria Cristina*) rewards bravery in battle and/or distinguished military service and was founded in 1890 in four classes (see illustration on page 9). Its naval equivalent is the *Royal and Naval Order of Maria Christina*, founded in the same year. The Badges are similar except that the former has the legend *Al merito en campana* ('For merit on campaign'), the latter *Al merito naval* ('For naval merit'). Meritorious (as opposed to gallant) service in Spain's armed forces is rewarded by the *Order of Military Merit* (*Orden del Militar*) (1864) and its naval equivalent, the *Order of Naval Merit* (*Orden del Merito Naval*) (1866), both instituted by Queen Isabella II and open to all ranks. In 1945, an equivalent for Spain's air forces was established in the form of the *Air Force Order of Merit*. All may be conferred on foreigners and have four classes.

A number of Orders were established specifically to reward distinguished service in various professions. They were all abolished on the formation of the republic in 1931 but re-established by Franco between 1939 and 1944. The *Order of the Cross of St Raimund de Peñaforte* (*Orden de la Cruz de San Raimundo de Peñaforte*) of 1944, awarded in five classes, was an award to members of the Spanish legal profession and is named after the patron saint of lawyers. The *Order of Civil Merit* (*Orden del Merito Civil*) (1926) was an award in six classes

(Left) Spain: Order of Military Merit. Knight's Breast Badge, c.1865. The award for war service has red enamel, while that for meritorious service in peacetime has white enamel. Obverse and reverse shown.

(Right) Spain: Breast Star of the Order of Charles III. The central medallion has an enamelled image of the Virgin Mary, taken for the 'Prado Madonna' by Morillo. Its motto is *Virtuti et Merito* ('for virtue and merit').

(Left) Spain: Order of Isabella the Second. Officer's Breast Badge in gold and enamels. Those awarded to non-officer ranks were in plain silver, without enamel.

(Right) Spain: Royal Order of Queen Maria Louisa. The attractive Breast Badge of this rarely awarded single-class Order. There is no Breast Star. The design features emblems of Castile and Leon between the arms of the cross, connected by a gold chain. In the centre is a fine depiction in enamel of St Ferdinand, who reigned as King Ferdinand at the time of the reunification of Spain in 1492.

for civil servants, whilst the *Civil Order of Public Health* (*Orden Civil de Sanidad*), established in 1922 and refounded in 1943, was conferred for distinguished service in the medical profession. In four classes, it could also be awarded to foreigners. The *Order of Agricultural Merit* (*Orden Civil del Merito Agricola*), founded by Alfonso XIII in 1905, rewarded outstanding contributions in the sphere of agriculture. It was re-established in four classes by Franco in 1942.

The *Civil Order of Alfonso XII* was established in 1902 to reward those who contributed to the cultural development of Spain. Abolished on the establishment of the Republic in 1931, it was replaced in 1939 by a new *Civil Order of Alfonso X, the Wise* (*Orden Civil de Alfonso X, El Sabio*). Named after Alfonso, known as 'the Wise', king of Castile and Leon from 1252 to 1284, it is awarded in five classes to artists, scientists, writers, teachers and others working in the sphere of culture.

The *Order of Cisneros* (*Orden de Cisneros*), named after Francis Cisneros (1436–1517), a famous prelate and royal advisor, was founded by Franco in 1944 to reward political loyalty and public service.

The *Royal Order of Queen Maria Louisa*, established in 1792, was an award for noble ladies who undertook significant charitable work.

COLONIAL AWARDS

Spain's principal colonial Orders were for service in its protectorate, the Kingdom of Morocco, and took the form of the *Order of Mehdaui*, established in 1926, and the *Order of Africa (Orden de Africa)*, established in 1933 for service to Spanish-African causes in general.

SWEDEN

The Baltic kingdom of Sweden, under the Vasa dynasty from 1521 to 1810, was one of the great powers of northern Europe and at various times united with Denmark and Norway. After the Napoleonic Wars, when Denmark was separated from the union, Sweden was left as the dominant power in the Kingdom of Norway and Sweden until Norway's secession in 1905. Sweden has since been an independent constitutional monarchy.

Since January 1975, only the Order of the Seraphim and the Order of the Pole Star may now be conferred and these only on foreigners or (since 1996) on members of the Royal Family. Two others, the Royal Order of the Sword and the Royal Order of Vasa, are regarded as dormant.

Sweden's Orders – most of which date from her earlier period as a great power rather than modern times – are distinctive and attractive.

The Order of the Name of Jesus, 1656
The Order of Amaranth, 1645
The Order of St Brigitta, 1366
The Order of the Alliance, 1527

(Left) Sweden: Most Noble Order of the Seraphim. Breast Star. The Order has only one class and membership is strictly limited. The arms of the star are linked by the winged faces of the seraphim.

(Right) Sweden: Royal Order of the Sword. This example of the Commander's Neck Badge by Carlman of Stockholm has crossed swords at the suspension and around the cross.

The Order of Mary Eleanor, 1632
The Order of the Lamb of God, 1564 (very short-lived)
The Most Noble Order of the Seraphim, 1260?, 1748, 1952
The Royal Order of the Sword, 1522 (in Livonia), 1748, 1952
The Royal Order of the Pole Star or *North Star*, 1748, 1952
The Royal Order of Vasa, 1772, 1952
The Order of Charles XIII, 1811 (an award only for Swedish Freemasons)

Sweden's most prestigious award is the beautiful *Most Noble Order of the Seraphim* (*Kungliga Seraphimerorden*), or 'Blue Ribbon', its equivalent of the English Order of the Garter. Re-established by Frederick I in 1748, it was claimed to resurrect an earlier (possibly apocryphal) version founded by King Magnus I in 1260. In one class, it was limited (in addition to the King and royal princes) to twenty-three Swedes whose outstanding service had already been recognised by the award of the Royal Order of the Sword or the Royal Order of the Pole Star, and to eight foreigners at any one time. When conferred for military service, crossed swords pierce the design. Associated with the Order is the *Seraphim Medal*, awarded for service to the poor and the sick.

(Left) Sweden: Royal Order of the Pole Star. Commander's Neck Badge with hinged crown suspension.

(Right) Sweden: Royal Order of Vasa. Knight's Breast Badge in silver-gilt and enamel, by Carlman of Stockholm.

The distinctive *Royal Order of the Sword* (*Kungliga Svärdsorden*), or 'Yellow Ribbon', was originally associated with the Teutonic Knights in the early thirteenth century and was re-established in 1522 by King Gustav I Vasa for award in Livonia. It was refounded as a Swedish military honour by Frederick I in 1748. Its five classes rewarded exceptionally long or meritorious service, essentially by officers. Its lower-tier awards, the *Badge of the Sword* and the *Medal of the Sword*, both created in 1850, are essentially long-service awards to lower ranks in the army. Another foundation of Frederick I in 1748 was the *Royal Order of the Pole Star* (*Kungliga Njordstärneorden*), the 'Black Ribbon', intended as a civil reward to distinguished civil servants, scientists, artists and clergymen. It could also be awarded to foreigners and had three classes after 1844.

The *Royal Order of Vasa* (*Kungliga Vasaorden*), or 'Green Ribbon', created in four classes by Gustav III in May 1772, was unusual in its day as being a reward for service in the fields of farming, art, mining, education, commerce and manufacture. The *Royal Badge of Vasa* and the *Royal Medal of Vasa*, in various grades, were conferred as lower-level awards.

SWITZERLAND

Established after 1291 as a confederation of provinces or *cantons* and as the Helvetic Republic in 1798, Switzerland has no Orders of Knighthood. Indeed, a Swiss citizen accepting a foreign Order is banned from holding any public appointment.

TURKEY

The Ottoman Empire and its successor, the Turkish Republic, are included in this survey because of Turkey's domination of the Balkans from the fifteenth century to the end of the nineteenth. Turkey retains an enclave in Europe to this day, comprising Istanbul and its hinterland.

Turkish Orders were established in imitation of the European system from the late eighteenth century, there being no hereditary Ottoman aristocracy and no tradition of such awards. Examples are often found in the medal groups of British officers who served in the Crimea (1854–56), Egypt (1882–88) and the Sudan (1884–98), or as awards to British officials serving in Egypt and the Sudan. Many were conferred on German officers during the First World War, when the Ottoman Empire was a German ally.

Imperial awards became obsolete on the formation of the Turkish Republic in 1922.

The Order of Merit, 1879–1922
The Order of Osmanieh, 1862–1922
The Order of the Crescent, 1799, 1801

(Left) Turkey: Order of Osmaniah. Breast Star of the Grand Cross, in silver, with gold and enamel centre. As with many Turkish Orders, this example was made in Paris (in this case by Krétly).

(Right) Turkey: Order of Mejidieh. Fifth Class Breast Badge.

The Order of Glory, 1831–52
The Order of Mejidieh, 1852–1922
The Order of Charity (or of Chastity), 1878–1922
The Order of Ertogreul, 1903
The Imperial Ottoman House Order, 1895
The Order of Merit of the Republic, 1924

(Left) Turkey: Order of Mejidieh. Neck Badge of the Third Class. It is of Turkish manufacture in silver with gold and enamel centre. The Breast Star is of essentially the same design.

(Right) Turkey: Order of Charity. Breast Badge of the Third Class, in silver, gold and enamel, with a beautifully enamelled wreath between the arms of the star. As is common with Turkish Orders, it has a 'star and crescent' suspension and bears the Sultan's cipher (toughra) in the centre. Its central inscription reads 'Humanity, charity and health'.

Turkey: Sultan's Gold Medal for Egypt, Third Class, 1801 (obverse and reverse). The three classes of this award (distinguished only by size) were essentially additional tiers to the existing Order of the Crescent (1799). Note the unusual chain and hook suspension.

The highest Turkish Order was the *Order of Merit* (*Nichan-el-Imtiaz*). Founded in only one class by Sultan Abdul Hamid in September 1879, it rewarded political, military and literary merit. It was also conferred, as a high honour, on members of the Royal Family, on foreign heads of state and on senior foreign officials. The Empire's second highest award was the *Order of Osmanieh*, created in January 1862 as an award for the most senior Turkish civil servants or to foreign nationals who had rendered exceptional service to the Sultan (see illustration on page 11).

The *Order of Glory* (*Nichan-el-Iftikhar*) was established in only one class by Sultan Mahmud II in August 1831 as a general reward for good service and was sometimes bestowed on foreigners. It was replaced in August 1852 by the *Order of Mejidieh* as a reward for special service to the Empire, military or civil. Both the *Osmanieh* and the *Mejidieh* were awarded in five classes and were frequently bestowed upon British officers (commonly in the third, fourth or fifth classes) for service in the Crimea in 1854–56, in Egypt in 1882 or in the Sudan between 1884 and 1910.

The *Order of the Crescent* was founded in two classes in 1799 largely to reward British and Turkish commanders in the war against Napoleon. It was extended by three more classes (commonly called the *Sultan's Gold Medal*) in 1801 following the British invasion of Egypt and the defeat of the French army of occupation. The award takes the form of a very thin gold medal in various sizes according to class, suspended from a gold chain and hook that was pinned to the jacket. The earlier (1799) versions, which became the higher grades of the 1801 foundation, were larger and usually decorated with jewels.

An unusual award was the *Order of Charity* (*Nichan-i-Shefkat*) (sometimes known as the *Order of Chastity*), founded in 1878 by Abdul Hamid II; in three classes, it was conferred only on women, Turkish and foreign, for charitable acts and, it is said, on ladies of the Sultan's harem!

After the fall of the Ottoman sultanate in 1918 and the Turkish revolution, imperial Orders were abolished. The *Order of Merit of the Republic* (1924) – also known simply as the *Independence Medal* – was granted to those who rendered exceptional service in the establishment of the new Republic, 1919–22.

Apart from this award, the Turkish Republic established no system of Orders.

UKRAINE

The province of Ukraine – 'the bread basket of Russia' – broke away from Russia after the 1917 revolution but Russian control was swiftly reimposed. In 1917, two Orders were established – the *Order of Freedom* and the *Order of the Archangel Gabriel*. As they were short-lived, few were awarded.

With the break-up of the Soviet Union, the Ukraine has again become an independent republic.

THE UNION OF SOVIET SOCIALIST REPUBLICS (USSR)

Established in 1922 after the fall of the Tsarist regime and the establishment of a communist republic, the USSR created a large number of Orders and Decorations, covering service in every walk of life, civil and military. Many used the ribbon colours of the old Tsarist awards, so that there was a degree of continuity between the old and new systems.

Most of these Orders, and a wide range created after 1945, effectively became obsolete following the break-up of the Soviet Union.

The Gold Star of Hero of the Soviet Union, 1924
The Gold Star of Hero of Socialist Labour, 1938
The Order of Lenin, 1930
The Order of the Red Banner, 1918
The Order of the Red Star, 1930
The Order of the Red Banner of Labour, 1928
The Order of the Badge of Honour, 1935
The Order of Suvarov, 1942

The Order of Kutuzov, 1942
The Order of Victory, 1943
The Order of Ushakov, 1944
The Order of Nakhimov, 1944
The Order of Bogdan Khmelnitsky, 1943
The Order of Alexander Nevsky, 1942
The Order of the Patriotic War, 1942
The Order of Glory, 1943
The Order of the Heroine Mother, 1944
The Order of the Glory of Motherhood, 1944

The new state's highest award was *Hero of the Soviet Union*. When it was instituted in 1924, the recipient received only a citation, but from 1939 a Badge was conferred. In one class, it takes the form of a plain five-pointed gold star and was awarded only for the most heroic or exceptional service, military or civil, to the USSR. It was conferred, for example, on the first astronaut, Yuri Gagarin, though most of its twenty thousand or so awards were made for gallantry during the Second World War; in military terms, it was effectively Russia's equivalent of the Victoria Cross. It could also be conferred on foreigners, one example being Fidel Castro. Recipients also received the Order of Lenin and the non-hereditary formal title 'Hero of the Soviet Union'.

(Left) USSR: Gold Star of Hero of the Soviet Union. In stark contrast to the elaborate designs of Tsarist awards, the simple gold star of the USSR's highest distinction must be the plainest of all high-ranking honours.

(Right) USSR: Order of Lenin. The single-class Badge is suspended like a medal from a red ribbon that has two narrow yellow stripes.

The *Hero of Socialist Labour* was established in 1938, its Badge conferred from 1940. Again in a single class, it was awarded for exceptional contribution to the modernisation of the USSR, i.e. achievements in industry, agriculture, science, technology and trade. Recipients received the non-hereditary formal title 'Hero of the Soviet Union' and also the Order of Lenin. As on many Soviet awards, the five-pointed gold star has the communist emblem, the hammer and sickle, set in the centre.

The Order of Lenin, established in April 1930 and named after the leader of the Bolshevik revolution, was the highest civil award in the USSR, granted for significant contribution to the state in any field. It could also be conferred on organisations and even factories. The Badge originally took the form of a gold and platinum plaque bearing a portrait of Lenin (1870–1924) surrounded by a wreath of rye in gold, but it was altered in 1931 (for example, by the addition of a red flag, bearing the name 'Lenin') and examples of the first version are rare.

The single-class *Order of the Red Banner* was a very early award, instituted in 1918, and conferred by the various republics constituting the USSR in their own versions. These were abolished in 1924 (and are now rare) and the award was standardised as a national Order. It was effectively a reward for conspicuous gallantry in action – many being awarded as such in the Second World War – but was sometimes granted for long and meritorious service in the forces. It could also be awarded as a 'unit citation' to entire regiments and formations. A version of this order 'for labour' was produced from 1928 for achievements in labour, production and factory work.

The *Order of the Red Star* was instituted in April 1930 as a military reward to all ranks and all Soviet forces for outstanding service in the defence of

(Left) USSR: Order of the Red Star. The screw-back Order bears as a central legend Marx's slogan 'Workers of the world unite' over *CCCP* ('USSR').

(Right) USSR: Red Star. Breast Badge, second type.

(Left) USSR: Order of the Red Banner of Labour. The numbered plaque – used on other Soviet awards – indicates that this is the recipient's fourth award of this honour. As is common with many Russian honours, these are individually numbered on the reverse.

(Right) USSR: Order of Victory. The single-class pocket Badge in platinum, gold, diamonds and enamel. This bejewelled Order is uncharacteristically showy for a Soviet award, but only eight were ever conferred. Its central medallion shows the Spassky Tower and the Kremlin.

the USSR; it could also be awarded to civilians (e.g. for life-saving) and to collective organisations and associations. Worn as a simple pocket badge, its five-pointed star in dark red enamel bore in the centre the image of a Red Army soldier, surrounded by the Marxist motto – 'Workers of the world unite'.

The *Order of the Badge of Honour* (November 1935) was conferred on civilians or collectives for production work in agriculture, industry, transport or commerce at a time when Russia was attempting a drastic and rapid modernisation. When given to military recipients, it was usually for training and organisational work rather than as a combat award. It took the form of an oval Breast Badge in red enamel, showing a man and woman in front of Soviet banners.

The Second World War created a need for a range of awards to recognise gallantry in action at different levels or exceptional service to the war effort. The magnificent *Order of Victory* (November 1943) was the USSR's highest purely military award. Worn only as a Breast Star, in platinum decorated with diamonds, it was conferred on the most senior commanders, Russian or foreign, for significant victories or advances. Only eight were ever conferred, all for 1939–45 service, two of them on the great Soviet commander, Marshal Zhukov. One was conferred on Field Marshal Montgomery and another on General Eisenhower. The *Order of Suvarov* (1942) had three classes, awarded according to the rank of the recipient, and represented only by a Breast Star. It was essentially for effective work in the organisation of military operations that resulted in the defeat of the enemy force engaged. It was named after Alexander, Count Suvarov (1729–1800), who rose from the ranks to become one of Russia's greatest generals of the eighteenth century. A slightly lower-tier military honour was the *Order of Kutuzov*, established in two classes in

(Left) USSR: Order of Suvarov. The screw-back Badge of the Second Class.

(Right) USSR: Order of Kutuzov. The screw-back Breast Badge of the Second Class. In silver and gold, with white and red enamel features, it bears a profile in gold of the famous Field Marshal (1745–1813). This level was awarded to Corps, Brigade and Divisional commanders.

July 1942 and extended to three in 1943. It was named after Russia's great general of the Napoleonic Wars, who, although defeated by Napoleon at Borodino, harried the French in their notorious retreat from Moscow in 1812. The Order, worn only as a Breast Star, bears Kutuzov's portrait and name. The *Order of Alexander Nevsky* – a title recalling the obsolete Tsarist award (q.v.), but dropping the title 'Saint' – celebrated one of Russia's greatest historical figures. Established in July 1942 in one class only, it was worn as a five-pointed Breast Star in red enamel and featuring a central portrait of the thirteenth-century hero on a base of crossed axes. It was conferred on officers of the Soviet army and air forces for bravery in combat or for leadership.

Possibly the most commonly awarded Russian Order for wartime service in any rank or branch of service and to partisans was the *Order of the Patriotic War* (May 1942). Granted for bravery in action or distinguished war service, it had two classes (one for combatants and one for non-combatants) and was awarded as a five-pointed red enamel star with gold or silver rays between the points, superimposed on which was the hammer and sickle emblem of the USSR, with the words 'Patriotic War'. Another award for bravery in battle was the *Order of Glory* (November 1943), open to all ranks from Lieutenant downward, and to all branches of the Soviet forces. It was awarded for such feats as killing between ten and fifty enemy soldiers, saving the life of an officer or disabling enemy tanks at close range. In three classes, it was worn only as a Breast Badge, using the ribbon of the old Order of St George, and featured the Spassky Tower and Kremlin surrounded by sprays of laurel above the word 'Glory'.

USSR: Order of Alexander Nevsky. The elaborate pin-back badge features a profile of the hero over the usual Soviet emblems – the hammer and sickle (signifying the unity of industry and agriculture) and the red star.

(Bottom left) USSR: Order of the Patriotic War, Second Class. Originally designed to hang from a ribbon, the design was altered to the usual screw-back badge. Unusually, it is worn on the *right* breast.

(Bottom right) USSR: Order of Glory. This is the First Class, in gold; the Second Class had a gold centre on a silver star, and the Third Class was all in silver. Unusually for Soviet Orders, it was worn from a ribbon, shown here folded in typical Russian fashion.

For the Other Ranks of the Soviet forces and wartime partisans, the *Order of Bogdan Khmelnitsky* (October 1943), conferred in three classes according to the rank of the recipient, rewarded distinguished service in action. The brainchild of Nikita Khrushchev as a Ukrainian general in 1943, it commemorated the Cossack leader Bogdan Khmelnitsky (1593–1657), who secured the allegiance of the Ukraine to the new Russian kingdom in 1649. Worn only as a ten-pointed Breast Star in gold and silver, it bore the hero's portrait and his name in Ukrainian script.

USSR: Order of Bogdan Khmelnitsky. The Second Class screw-back badge, with gold centre on silver rays. The First Class has the rays in gold and silver, and the Third Class is entirely in silver.

(Left) USSR: Order of Ushakov. The screw-back pocket Badge, Second Class.

(Right) USSR: Order of Nakhimov. The screw-back pocket Badge, First Class. The Second Class has the background rays in silver and the central medallion is not enamelled.

Two wartime awards honoured service in the Soviet navy. The *Order of Ushakov* (March 1944), the USSR's highest purely naval reward, came in two classes and was conferred for the successful planning and implementation of naval operations leading to the defeat of the enemy force. It was named after Admiral Feodor Ushakov (1744–1817), a naval commander famous for his successes against the Turks. The award, a five-pointed platinum Breast Star, bears Ushakov's portrait and name in the centre, over a naval anchor. The *Order of Nakhimov* (March 1944), a six-pointed Breast Star in silver and blue enamel bearing the central portrait of Admiral Nakhimov (1802–55),

rewarded distinguished service in the planning and implementation of naval operations. In two classes, its First Class was awarded only to Admirals and its Second Class to other naval officers.

Two unusual awards, both created in July 1944, were the *Order of the Heroine Mother*, granted with the formal title 'Mother Heroine' to women who bore and raised ten or more children, and the *Order of the Glory of Motherhood*, to mothers who raised large families. The former was a single-class gold star on a silver rayed plaque, suspended from a brooch bearing the words 'Mother Heroine'. The latter came in three classes and took the form of an oval plaque in silver showing a mother holding a child, next to a red banner inscribed 'Glory of Motherhood'. The badge hung from an enamel bow in white and blue.

THE VATICAN

The Vatican – now the world's smallest sovereign state, established in the heart of Rome – was formerly the centre of a temporal power, the Papal or Roman States. Like any secular Italian state, the Papal States had a system of Orders, some dating back to the early Middle Ages. As the hub of the modern Catholic Church, the Vatican still awards some of its historic Orders and modern equivalents for service to the Papacy and the Church of Rome. The Papal system of Orders was remodelled by Pope Pius X in 1905.

The insignia are generally attractive and well made, being produced in a number of countries.

> *The Order of Christ*, 1319, 1905
> *The Order of St Gregory the Great*, 1831, 1905
> *The Order of Pius*, 1847, 1905, 1957
> *The Order of St Sylvester*, 1841, 1905
> *The Order of the Knights of the Holy Sepulchre*, 1099?, 1496, 1868
> *The Order of the Golden Spur*, 330?, 1539–1841, 1905
> *The Order of the Moor*, 1806
> *The Order of St Cecilia*, 1847
> *The Cross Pro Ecclesia et Pontifice*, 1888 and 1908
> *The Award Bene Merenti of Pius XI*, 1925
> *The Lateran Cross of the Knights of St John* (or *Order of St John of Lateran*), 1903
> *The Order of the Advocates of Peter*, 1877

The Order of Christ (*Ordine Supremo del Christo*) began as a branch of the Knights Templars. After their dissolution in 1312, a section remained in Portugal under the title of the Order of Christ, its existence confirmed by the Pope in 1319. The insignia of the Order then became both a Portuguese and a

(Left) Vatican: Order of the Knights of the Holy Sepulchre. Commander's Neck Badge, in silver-gilt and enamel. The Order's Knights originally claimed precedence over all other Orders except the Golden Fleece. The elaborate Badge is a 'Jerusalem cross' – a cross potent with four Greek crosses in the angles.

(Right) Vatican: Order of St Sylvester. The Collar Chain and pendant Badge of the Grand Cross (i.e. First Class).

Papal honour, conferred by both states to this day. In only one class, Knight, the Order of Christ is the highest-ranking Papal Order. Rarely conferred, it is granted only to heads of state and those who have rendered outstanding service to the Church or society in general. Only one Protestant has received the award – Count Otto von Bismarck in 1885.

According to tradition, the *Order of the Knights of the Holy Sepulchre* was founded by Godfrey de Bouillon at Jerusalem during the First Crusade (1095–99). It is more securely dated to 1496, when a military Order was established by Pope Alexander VI for the protection of the Holy Sepulchre. It was reorganised into its present three classes in 1868 and is awarded for charitable and cultural achievements.

The *Order of the Golden Spur (Ordine dello Speron d'Oro)* has been claimed to date from the fourth century but was certainly in existence by 1559, when it was confirmed as a military Order by Paul IV. In 1841 it was re-established by Gregory XVI as the *Order of St Sylvester* (after its supposed fourth-century founder) and was further reformed in 1905, when it was reconstituted as a single-class Order of the Golden Spur or Golden Legion (*Milizia Aurata*). Conferred only under the direct instigation of the Pope himself, it is the highest award for non-Catholics, conferred for special service to the Church or in its defence, and restricted to only one hundred Knights at any time.

(Left) Vatican: Order of Pius. Grand Cross (i.e. First Class) set, by Bertarelli of Rome, Sash Badge with Sash and Breast Star.

(Right) Vatican: Order of St Gregory the Great. Knight's Breast Badge, by Halley of Paris, in fitted case.

Founded by Pius IX in 1847, the *Order of Pius* (*Ordine Piano* or *Ordo Pianus*) commemorates Pope Pius IV, who founded a short-lived *Ordo Pianus* in 1559. It was reorganised in 1905 and 1957 and is usually conferred for personal services to the Pope and Papacy. It has four classes. Since 1929 the Badge has been worn from a Collar and with a Breast Star.

The *Order of St Gregory the Great* (*Ordine di San Gregorio Magno*) was instituted in 1831 by Gregory XVI, originally to reward loyal service to the Papal States by Austrian forces and local citizens during the disturbances of 1830. Named after Pope Gregory I (590–604), the Order was reorganised in 1905 and has both military and civil divisions, each in three classes, conferred for loyalty, zeal and meritorious service.

YUGOSLAVIA

The Treaty of St Germain in 1919 established the Kingdom of Yugoslavia around the Kingdom of Serbia as the dominant partner in an amalgamation of several Balkan areas. Under German occupation from 1941 to 1945, Yugoslavia became a communist 'People's Republic' under Marshal Tito in 1945. Following the Balkan Wars of the 1990s, the territories of 'Former Yugoslavia' separated into a number of independent republics, including a new Serbia.

Some of Serbia's former Orders – the Order of the Star of Karageorge, the

Order of the White Eagle and the Order of St Sava (q.v.) – remained in use in Yugoslavia in its early years. Like other communist states, it later awarded a wide range of Orders and Decorations for service in all walks of life.

The Order of the Crown, 1929–45
The Order of Freedom, 1945
The Order of the National Hero, 1943
The Order for National Liberation, 1943
The Order for Valour, 1943
The Order of Labour with the Red Banner, 1945
The Order of Brotherhood and Unity, 1945
The Order of the Partisan Star 'with Gold Wreath', 1943
The Order of Service (or Merit) to the People, 1945

Yugoslavia: Order
of the Crown.
Breast Badge.

The only Order established in Yugoslavia between the world wars was the *Order of the Crown* (*Orden Krune*), founded in October 1929 by Alexander I in honour of his father, Peter I. Awarded for civil and military merit, it had three classes. Following the overthrow of the monarchy in 1945, the Royal Family in exile under Peter II continued to award the Order up to 1970.

A new range of Orders was created by Marshal Josef Tito, commander of Yugoslavia's communist partisan forces, in the latter years of the war. An example is the *Order for Valour* (*Orden za Hrabrost*), awarded from March 1943 (along with a lower-tier *Medal of Valour*) to all ranks and civilians for bravery in battle. When Tito established the communist republic in November 1945, these Orders remained as national awards.

The *Order of Freedom* (*Orden Sloboda*), in one class and worn only as a Breast Star, was Yugoslavia's highest military honour, established in 1945 for outstanding leadership or gallantry. The *Order of National Hero* (*Orden Narodnog Heroja*), awarded from 1943 under similar circumstances but perhaps at a lesser level, entitled the recipient to the formal title 'Hero'. It too had only one class, but was worn as a Breast Badge from a ribbon. The *Order for National Liberation* (*Orden Narodnog Oslobodjenja*), again established only as a single-class Breast Star, was awarded to partisans and citizens for bravery in actively resisting the German occupation, as was the *Order of the Partisan Star* (*Orden Partiszanske Zvezde*), which had three classes.

Yugoslavia: Order of the National Hero. The Badge, worked in gold, is borne on a ribbon of red with a narrow white stripe towards each edge. The Order's one class entitles the recipient to the formal title 'Hero'.

Yugoslavia: Order of the Partisan Star, founded in 1943 in three classes by Marshal Joseph Broz Tito. Yugoslavia's post-1943 Orders are very similar in design to those of the Soviet bloc, using the familiar images and emblems of the communist nations of that time, although Yugoslavia under Tito was not formally part of the bloc.

FURTHER READING

There is a large and growing literature on European Orders, including regional and national studies and detailed monographs on individual Orders. Most are, understandably, produced by experts in their own country and in their own language and it is quite common to find that there are no or few studies in English of the Orders even of some major states. The list below contains only the more accessible modern works in English. Many of the older, detailed works on specific Orders are collectors' items in their own right.

The serious researcher wishing to find a detailed study in a country's own language should consult the *Bibliography of Orders and Decorations* by C. P. Mulder and A. A. Purves (Ordenshistorik Selskab, Copenhagen, 1999).

The Internet also offers the opportunity to find information on European Orders; just typing in the name of the Order will produce results in most cases.

GENERAL

The Statutes of the various Orders.

Dorling, H. Tapprell. *Ribbons and Medals*. London, revised and enlarged edition 1983. A selective but useful survey of British and foreign awards.

Hieronymussen, P. O. *Orders, Medals and Decorations of Britain and Europe in Colour*. London, 1967.

Mericka, V. *Orders and Decorations*. London, 1967.

Mericka, V. *The Book of Orders and Decorations*. London, 1976. A very useful and informative book.

Purves, A. A. *Orders and Decorations*. London, 1972. An attractive paperback guide.

Purves, A. A. *Collecting Medals and Decorations*. London, 1983. A useful handbook.

Purves, A. A. *The Medals, Decorations and Orders of World War Two, 1939–45*. London, 1986.

Purves, A. A. *The Medals, Decorations and Orders of the Great War, 1914–18*. London, 1989.

Rossignoli, G. *Ribbons of Orders, Decorations and Medals*. London, 1976.

Werlich, R. *Orders and Decorations of All Nations*. Washington, 1974. The standard catalogue.

NATIONAL

Acovic, D. M. *Orders, Decorations and Medals of Bulgaria*. Beograd, 1977.

Angolia, J. *For Führer and Fatherland: Military Awards of the Third Reich* (several volumes). California, 1976–80.

Bascapé, G. *The Orders of Knighthood and the Nobility of the Republic of San Marino*. Delft, 1973.

Bere, Sir I. de la. *The Queen's Orders of Chivalry*. London, 1961. British Orders.

Blondel, J. M. *Orders of the Imperial German States*. Privately published, 1987.

Bossé, J. R. S. de. *The Orders, Decorations and Medals of the Principalities of Liechtenstein, Monaco and the Republic of San Marino*. Luxembourg, 1953.

Brunschwig, R. *The Legion of Honour*. Paris, 1968.

Dimacoupolos, G. D. *Greek Orders and Medals*. Athens, 1961.

Duckers, P. *British Orders and Decorations*. Shire, Princes Risborough, 2004.

Duren, P. B. van. *The Cross and the Sword*. Gerrards Cross, 1987. Papal Orders, etc.

Duren, P. B. van. *Orders of Knighthood and Merit*. Gerrards Cross, 1995. Papal and Catholic Orders.

Durov, V. A. *Russian and Soviet Orders*. Moscow, 1977.

Durov, V. A. *The Orders of Russia*. Moscow, 1993.

Edkins, D. *The Prussian Ordern pour le Mérite – The History of the Blue Max*. Virginia, 1981.

Engel, C. E. *Knights of Malta*. London, 1963.

Erufen and Tarihi. *Turkish Orders and Medals*. Istanbul, 1979. The definitive study.

Falkenstein, J. von. *Imperial Austrian Medals and Decorations*. Florida, 1972.

Gillingham, H. E. *Ephemeral Decorations*. New York, 1935.

Gillingham, H. E. *Spanish Orders of Chivalry and Decorations of Honour*. New York, 1967.

Grundmanis, Z. *Orders and Decorations of Latvia, 1919–40*. Ontario, 1975.

Hannes, W. *Orders of Estonia*. Tallinn, 1996.

Jørgensen, P. J. *Danish Orders and Medals*. Copenhagen, 1964.

Kavaliauskas, V. *Poland: Military Medals and Decorations, 1638–1940*. Toronto, 1980.

Kozlowski, M., and Furklan, M. *Czechoslovakia Military Medals and Decorations*. Toronto, 1987.

McDaniel, P., and Schmitt, P. J. *The Comprehensive Guide to Soviet Orders and Decorations*. Arlington, 1997.

Meijer, H. G., Mulder, C. P., and Wagenaar, B. W. *Orders and Decorations of the Netherlands*. Venlo, 1984.

Neville, D. G. *Medal Ribbons and Orders of Imperial Germany and Austria*. St Ives, 1974.

Pashkov, P. *The White Armies' Orders and Badges of the Civil War, 1917–22*. Akron, 1983.

Pichel, T. *History of the Sovereign Order of St John of Jerusalem, Knights of Malta*. Pennsylvania, 1957.

Prowse, A. E. *The Iron Cross of Prussia and Germany.* New Zealand, 1971.

Romanoff, Prince D. *The Orders, Medals and History of Montenegro.* Copenhagen, 1980.

Romanoff, Prince D. *The Orders, Medals and History of the Kingdom of Bulgaria.* Ryngsted Kyst, 1982.

Romanoff, Prince D. *The Orders, Medals and History of Greece.* Ryngsted Kyst, 1987.

Romanoff, Prince D. *The Orders, Medals and History of Imperial Russia.* Ryngsted Kyst, 1987.

Scandaluzzi, F. *Ribbons of the Orders, Decorations and Medals of the Vatican, Sovereign Order of Malta, Liechtenstein, Monaco, San Marino and Luxembourg.* Milan, 1995.

Shoviera, J. *Slovakia: Decorations and Insignia, 1938–45.* Toronto, 1994.

Tammann, G. A. *Imperial Russian Makers' Marks on Orders and Decorations.* London, 1993.

Tetri, J. E. *Orders, Decorations and Medals of Finland.* Privately published, undated. In Finnish, with English sections.

Tozer, C. W. *The Insignia and Medals of the Grand Priory of the Most Venerable Order of the Hospital of St John of Jerusalem.* London, 1975.

Veldt, J. van der. *The Ecclesiastical Orders of Knighthood.* Washington, 1968.

Vos, R. de. *History of the Monies, Medals and Tokens of Monaco, 1640–1977.* Monaco, 1977.

Weber, P. M. *The Order of St Sava* (Serbia). Chicago, 1971.

Werlich, R. *Russian Orders, Decorations and Medals, including those of Imperial Russia, the Provisional Government and the Soviet Union.* Washington, 1982.

Wesolowksi, Z. P. *Polish Orders, Medals, Badges and Insignia, Military and Civilian, 1705–1985.* Miami, 1986.

Williamson, G. *The Iron Cross, A History, 1813–1957.* Poole, 1985.

COLLECTING ORDERS AND DECORATIONS

For those wishing to collect European Orders, the major London auction houses are the best source. The following firms issue regular auction catalogues and frequently offer a good range of European Orders:

Morton & Eden, 45 Maddox Street, London W1S 2PE.
  Telephone: 020 7493 5344.
  Email: info@mortonandeden.com
  Website: www.mortonandeden.com
DNW, 16 Bolton Street, Piccadilly, London W1J 8BQ.
  Telephone: 020 7016 1700.
  Website: www.dnw.co.uk
Spink & Son, 69 Southampton Row, Bloomsbury, London WC1B 4ET.
  Telephone: 020 7563 4000.
  Email: info@spink.com
  Website: www.spink-online.com

INDEX

Academic Palms (France) 10, 32
Adolph of Nassau (Luxembourg) 58, 59, 60
Advocates of Peter (Vatican) 103
Aeronautical Merit (Romania) 74
Africa (Spain) 87, 91
African Star (Belgium) 20, 21
Agricultural Merit (France) 32, 35
Agricultural Merit (Romania) 74, 76
Agricultural Merit (Spain) 87, 90
Alcantara (Spain) 87
Alexander Nevsky (USSR) 97, 100, 101
Alfonso X (Spain) 86, 90
Alfonso XII (Spain) 87, 90
Alliance (Sweden) 91
Annunciation (Italy) 6, 52, 53
Archangel Gabriel (Ukraine) 96
Badge of Honour (USSR) 96, 99
Bath (Great Britain) 41, 43
Bene Merenti (Vatican) 103
Black Eagle (Prussia) 71, 72
Black Star of Benin (France) 36
Blood Order (Nazi Germany) 38
Bogdan Khmelnitsky (USSR) 97, 101, 102
British Empire (Great Britain) 11, 41, 44, 45
British India (Great Britain) 41, 46
Brotherhood and Unity (Yugoslavia) 106
Calatrava (Spain) 87
Carol I (Romania) 74, 75
Charity or Chastity (Ottoman Turkey) 94, 96
Charity (Spain) 87
Charles III (Spain) 86, 88, 89
Charles IV (Czechoslovakia) 25, 26
Charles XIII (Sweden) 92
Christ (Portugal) 68, 69
Christ (Vatican) 103, 104
Cisneros (Spain) 87, 90
Civil Merit (Bulgaria) 22, 23
Civil Merit (Italy) 55
Civil Merit (Spain) 87, 89
Civil Order of Savoy (Italy) 55
Companions of Honour (Great Britain) 41, 47
Concord (Prussia) 71
Crescent (Ottoman Turkey) 93, 95, 96
Cross of Liberty (Estonia) 28, 29
Cross of Liberty (Finland) 29, 30
Cross of Merit (Latvia) 56
Cross of Merit (Malta) 61
Cross of Vytis (Lithuania) 57, 58
Cross with Eagle (Estonia) 29
Crown (Belgium) 19, 21
Crown (Monaco) 62
Crown (Romania) 11
Crown (Yugoslavia) 106, 107
Crown of India (Great Britain) 41, 46
Crown of Italy (Italy) 53, 54
Crown of King Zvonimir (Croatia) 24, 25
Crown of Prussia (Prussia) 37, 71, 73
Crown of Romania (Romania) 74, 75
Cultural Merit (Monaco) 62
Culture and Freedom (Romania) 75
Danilo (Montenegro) 62, 63, 64
Dannebrog (Denmark) 10, 27
Decoration of Honour for Merit (Austria) 15, 19
Distinguished Service Order (Great Britain) 41, 44
Dragon of Assam (France) 36
Eagle with Crown (Bohemia) 21
Elephant (Denmark) 27
Elizabeth (Romania) 75
Elizabeth Theresa (Austria) 16, 18
Empire (Portugal) 68, 71
Ermine (France) 31
Faithful Service (Romania) 74, 76
Falcon of Stefanik (Czechoslovakia) 25, 26
Ferdinand I (Romania) 74, 76
Finnish Lion (Finland) 29, 30, 31
Fleur-de-Lys (France) 32, 34
France I of Austria 17
Francis Joseph I (Austria) 15, 17, 18

Freedom (Czechoslovakia) 25
Freedom (Ukraine) 96
Freedom (Yugoslavia) 106, 107
Garter (Great Britain) 27, 32, 41, 42, 53, 92
Generosity (Prussia) 71, 72
George I (Greece) 48, 49
German Cross (Nazi Germany) 38, 40
German Eagle (Nazi Germany) 38, 39
German Order (Nazi Germany) 38
Glory (Ottoman Turkey) 94, 95
Glory (USSR) 97, 100, 101
Glory of Motherhood (USSR) 97, 103
Golden Angel or St George (Italy) 52
Golden Fleece (Burgundy, Austria, Spain) 15, 16, 23, 27, 53, 86, 87, 88
Golden Lion of Nassau (Luxembourg) 58, 59
Golden Spur (Hungary) 50, 51
Golden Spur (Vatican) 103, 104
Grand Duke Gediminas (Lithuania) 57, 58
Grimaldi (Monaco) 62
Grünwald Cross (Poland) 66, 67
Hero of Socialist Labour (USSR) 96, 98
Hero of Soviet Union (USSR) 96, 97
Heroine Mother (USSR) 97, 103
Hohenzollern (Prussia) 9, 71, 73
Hohenzollern (Romania) 74, 76
Holland (Netherlands) 63
Holy Crown of St Stephen (Hungary) 51
Holy Ghost or Holy Spirit (France) 12, 31, 32
Holy Sepulchre (Vatican) 103, 104
Holy Vial (France) 31, 32
House of Orange (Netherlands) 63, 65
Hungarian Order of St Stephen (Hungary) 50, 51
Hunting Order of St Hubert (Bohemia) 21
Icelandic Falcon (Iceland) 51
Independence (Montenegro) 62
Indian Empire (Great Britain) 41, 45, 46
Indian Order of Merit (Great Britain) 41, 46
Industrial & Agricultural Merit (Portugal) 68, 70, 71
Iron Cross (Prussia and Germany) 37, 38, 39, 40, 71
Iron Crown (France, Italy & Austria) 15, 17, 32, 34, 35
Iron Trefoil (Croatia) 24, 25
Isabella II (Spain) 87, 90
Isabella the Catholic (Spain) 86, 88, 89
Johanniter Order (Prussia) 61
Jubilee Brethren (Italy) 52
Karageorge Star (Serbia) 11, 83, 84, 105
Knight's Cross of Iron Cross (Nazi Germany) 39, 40
Knights of St Agatha (San Marino) 81
Kutuzov (USSR) 96, 99, 100
Labour with Red Banner (Yugoslavia) 106
Lacplesis the Bear Slayer (Latvia) 56, 57
Lateran Cross (Vatican) 103
Legion of Honour (France) 5, 31, 32, 33, 34
Lenin (USSR) 96, 98
Leopold (Austria) 15, 17
Leopold (Belgium) 19, 20
Liberation (France) 32, 35
Lily (Italy) 52
Lily or Fleur-de-Lys (France) 32, 34
Louise (Prussia) 71, 72
Loyalty (France) 32
Malta (Malta) 60, 61
Mannerheim Cross (Finland) 10, 29, 30
Maria Christina (Spain) 9, 86, 89
Maria Louis (Spain) 87, 90
Maria Victoria (Spain) 87
Maria Theresa (Austria) 15, 16
Maritime Merit (France) 31
Mary Eleanor (Sweden) 92
Matilda (Denmark) 27
Mehdaui (Spain) 91
Mejidieh (Ottoman Turkey) 94, 95
Merit (Courland) 24

Merit (Croatia) 24, 25
Merit (Great Britain) 41, 47
Merit (Hungary) 51
Merit (Netherlands) 63
Merit (Ottoman Turkey) 93, 95
Merit (Portugal) 68, 71
Merit (Romania) 74
Merit for Labour (Italy) 55
Merit for Science and Arts (Romania) 74, 76
Merit in Commerce (France) 31
Merit of Indo China (France) 36
Merit of the Crown of Prussia (Prussia) 71, 73
Merit of the Principality (Liechtenstein) 57
Merit of the Republic (Turkey) 94, 96
Merit of the Spanish Republic (Spain) 87
Michael the Brave (Romania) 74
Military Merit (Austria) 7, 16
Military Merit (Bulgaria) 22
Military Merit (France) 31, 33
Military Merit (Italy) 53, 54
Military Merit (Spain) 86, 89
Military Order of Savoy or Italy (Italy) 53, 54, 55
Military Virtue (Poland) 11, 66, 67
Milos the Great (Serbia) 82, 83
Nakhimov (USSR) 97, 102, 103
National Guard (Latvia) 56
National Hero (Yugoslavia) 106, 107
National Liberation (Yugoslavia) 106, 107
National Order of France (France) 31, 32
Naval Merit (Spain) 86, 88
Netherlands Lion (Netherlands) 63, 64, 65
Norwegian Lion (Norway) 65
Oaken Crown (Luxembourg) 58, 59, 60
Orange-Nassau (Netherlands) 63, 64, 65
Order of Freedom (Finland) 29, 30
Osmanieh (Ottoman Turkey) 11, 93, 94, 95
Ottoman House Order (Ottoman Turkey) 94
Our Lady of Montesa (Spain) 87
Our Lady of Villa Vicosa (Portugal) 68, 70
Partisan Star (Yugoslavia) 106, 107
Patriotic War (USSR) 97, 100, 101
Perfect Unity (Denmark) 27
Phoenix (Greece) 48, 49
Pius (Vatican) 103, 105
Pole Star (Sweden) 5, 9, 92, 93
Polonia Restituta (Poland) 66, 67
Pour le Merite (Prussia) 71, 72, 73
Prince Pribina (Slovakia) 85
Pro Ecclesia et Pontifice (Vatican) 103
Provincial Guard (Romania) 75
Public Health (France) 31
Public Health (Spain) 87
Public Instruction (Portugal) 68, 71
Red Banner (USSR) 96, 98
Red Banner of Labour (USSR) 96, 98
Red Eagle (Prussia) 10, 37, 71, 72, 73
Red Star (USSR) 96, 98, 99
Redeemer (Greece) 6, 48
Reunion (France) 32, 34, 35
Roman Eagle (Italy) 55
Royal Cambodian Order (France) 36
Royal Crown (Italy) 52
Royal Family Order (Great Britain) 41, 46
Royal Military Order for Bravery in War (Bulgaria) 22, 23
Royal Order of the Lion (Belgium) 20
Royal Order of Union (Netherlands) 63
Royal Victorian Chain (Great Britain) 41, 47
Royal Victorian Order (Great Britain) 41, 47
St Alexander (Bulgaria) 22, 23
St Alexander Nevsky (Russia) 12, 77, 78
St Andrew (Russia) 12, 77, 78
St Anne (Russia) 5, 7, 9, 12, 13, 77, 78, 79
St Anthony of Hainault (Austria) 15
St Benedict of Aviz (Portugal) 68, 69
St Brigitta (Sweden) 91
St Catherine (Russia) 77, 80, 81
St Cecilia (Vatican) 103

St Charles the Holy (Monaco) 61, 62
St Elizabeth (Austria) 16, 18, 19
St Ferdinand (Spain) 86, 87, 88, 89
St George (Austria) 15
St George (Romania) 75
St George (Russia) 77, 79, 80, 81, 100
St Gregory the Great (Vatican) 103, 105
St Hermengildo (Spain) 86, 88
St Hubert of Lorraine & Bar (France) 31, 33
St Isabella (Portugal) 68, 70
St James of the Sword (Portugal) 68, 69, 70
St James of the Sword (Spain) 87
St John of Jerusalem (various) 41, 85, 87
St Lazarus (Czechoslovakia) 25
St Lazarus (Serbia) 82, 83
St Lazarus & Our Lady of Mt. Carmel (France) 8
St Lazarus of Jerusalem (France) 31, 32
St Louis (France) 31, 33
St Marinus or Marino (San Marino) 81
St Michael (France) 31, 32, 33
St Michael and St George (Great Britain) 41, 44
St Michael the Brave (Romania) 6, 74, 76
St Nicholas, Creator of Peace (Russia) 76
St Olaf (Norway) 65
St Patrick (Great Britain) 41, 42, 43
St Peter (Montenegro) 62, 63
St Raimund de Penaforte (Spain) 86, 89
St Sava (Serbia) 82, 84, 106
St Stanislaus (Poland) 66, 67
St Stanislas (Russia) 9, 77, 79
St Stephen (Austria) 15, 16, 17
St Sylvester (Vatican) 103, 104
St Vladimir (Russia) 12, 37, 77, 80, 81
Sts Cyril and Methodius (Bulgaria) 22, 23
Sts George and Constantine (Greece) 48, 49
Sts Maurice and Lazarus (Italy) 53, 54
Sts Olga and Sophia (Greece) 48, 49
Seraphim (Sweden) 91, 92
Service to the People (Yugoslavia) 106
Sincerity (Prussia) 71, 72
Skanderberg (Albania) 15
Slovak Cross (Slovakia) 85
Social Service (France) 31
Sophia Magdalena (Denmark) 27
Star (France) 31
Star of Anjouan (France) 36
Star of India (Great Britain) 41, 45, 46
Star of Italy (Italy) 55
Star of Romania (Romania) 74, 75
Starry Cross (Austria) 16, 18
Suvarov (USSR) 97, 99, 100
Sword (Sweden) 5, 9, 10, 91, 92, 93
Takovo (Serbia) 82, 84
Teutonic Knights 29
Thistle (Great Britain) 41, 42
Three Stars (Latvia) 56
Tower and Sword (Portugal) 68, 69
Unification (Romania) 75
Ushakov (USSR) 97, 102
Valour (Yugoslavia) 106, 107
Vasa (Sweden) 7, 92, 93
Vesthardus (Latvia) 56, 57
Victoria and Albert (Great Britain) 41, 46, 47
Victorious War Cross (Slovakia) 85
Victory (USSR) 97, 99
Vitez (Hungary) 50, 51
Vytautas the Great (Lithuania) 57, 58
White Eagle (Poland) 66, 67
White Eagle (Russia) 12, 77
White Eagle (Serbia) 11, 82, 106
White Lion (Czechoslovakia) 25, 26
White Lion 'for Victory' (Czechoslovakia) 25, 26
White Rose (Finland) 10, 29, 31
White Star (Estonia) 29
Wilhelm (Prussia) 71, 73
William (Netherlands) 63, 64
Yoke and Arrows (Spain) 86, 88